SCOTTISH
COOKERY

This edition published in 2012 for Lomond Books Ltd
Broxburn, EH52 5NF, Scotland
www.lomondbooks.com

Publisher's Note:

Raw or semi-cooked eggs should not be consumed by babies, toddlers, pregnant
or breast-feeding women, the elderly or those suffering from a recurring illness.

Publisher & Creative Director: Nick Wells
Senior Project Editor: Catherine Taylor
Art Director: Mike Spender
Layout Design: Vanessa Green
Digital Design & Production: Chris Herbert

Created by and copyright © 2010 Flame Tree Publishing
Flame Tree is part of the Foundry Creative Media Company Limited
www.flametreepublishing.com

13 14 12
3 5 7 9 10 8 6 4 2

ISBN: 978-1-84204-218-2

A copy of the CIP data for this book is available from the British Library.

Printed in China

Front cover image (Eilean Donan Castle): © Joel Santos/Aurora/Getty Images.
Back cover image (Loch Katrine): © Joe Cornish/Dorling Kindersley/Getty Images.

All images © Foundry Arts, except:
Courtesy of iStock: 12 © george jurasek. Courtesy of Shutterstock: 6 & 11, 32, 79, 86, 84 & 89, 94,
100 & 120 © Monkey Business Images; 108 © Paul Cowan; 34 © William Berry. Courtesy of Stock Food:
10 © FoodPhotogr.Eising; 78 © Jonathan Gregson. Courtesy of WikimediaCommons/IMBJR 121

breakfasts

A good hearty Scottish breakfast is the ideal way to start the morning, especially if your day involves energetic outdoor activities. Oats take many forms, from a warming dish of oatmeal porridge to a plate of oatcakes. Smoked fish, such as smoked haddock and salmon, is also popular, especially when made into a tasty kedgeree. The national favourite, black pudding, is a traditional breakfast staple, often served with eggs, bacon and Scottish morning rolls, a special breakfast bread enjoyed with jam or marmalade.

Left: Smoked fish, such as Arbroath smokies, eggs and home-made bread or bannocks, form the heart of the traditional Scottish breakfast.

porridge

One of Scotland's oldest foods, oatmeal porridge remains a favourite way to start the day, especially during winter or when you are about to go out for a day's walking on the hills. Brown sugar or honey, cream and a tot of whisky are treats added for weekend breakfasts. Serve with stewed plums for a low-fat breakfast.

1 Put the water, pinhead oatmeal and salt into a heavy pan and bring the mixture to the boil over a medium heat, stirring with a wooden spatula. When the porridge is smooth and beginning to thicken, reduce the heat to a simmer.

2 Cook over a gentle heat for about 25 minutes, stirring occasionally, until the oatmeal is cooked and the consistency smooth.

3 Serve hot with cold milk or cream and extra salt, if required.or with stewed plums and sugar or honey.

Variation
Modern rolled oats can be used, in the proportion of 115g/4oz/ generous 1 cup to 750ml/1¼ pints/3 cups water, plus a sprinkling of salt. This cooks more quickly than pinhead oatmeal. Simmer, stirring to prevent sticking, for about 5 minutes. Either type of oatmeal can be left to cook overnight in the slow oven of a range.

Serves 4

1 litre/1¾ pints/4 cups water
115g/4oz/1 cup pinhead oatmeal
good pinch of salt
stewed plums or single (light) cream
  with sugar or honey, to serve

Per portion Energy 115kcal/488kJ; Protein 3.6g; Carbohydrate 20.9g, of which sugars 0g; Fat 2.5g, of which saturates 0g; Cholesterol 0mg; Calcium 16mg; Fibre 2g; Sodium 304mg.

SCOTTISH COOKERY

DELICIOUS CONTEMPORARY & CLASSIC
STEP-BY-STEP RECIPES

LOMOND

CONTENTS

SOUPS, STARTERS & SNACKS

Swede, Turnip, Parsnip & Potato Soup

2 large onions, peeled

25 g/1 oz butter

2 medium carrots, peeled
and roughly chopped

175 g/6 oz swede, peeled
and roughly chopped

125 g/4 oz turnip, peeled
and roughly chopped

125 g/4 oz parsnip, peeled
and roughly chopped

175 g/6 oz potatoes, peeled

1 litre/1¾ pints vegetable stock

½ tsp freshly grated nutmeg

salt and freshly ground black pepper

4 tbsp vegetable oil, for frying

125 ml/4 fl oz double cream

warm crusty bread, to serve

HELPFUL HINT

For a lower-fat version of this delicious
soup, add milk (skimmed if preferred)
rather than cream when reheating.

Finely chop 1 onion. Melt the butter in a large saucepan and add the onion, carrots, swede, turnip, parsnip and potatoes. Cover and cook gently for about 10 minutes, without colouring. Stir occasionally during this time.

Add the stock and season to taste with the nutmeg, salt and pepper. Cover and bring to the boil, then reduce the heat and simmer gently for 15–20 minutes, or until the vegetables are tender. Remove from the heat and leave to cool for 30 minutes.

Thinly slice the remaining onion. Heat the oil in a large heavy-based frying pan. Add the onion and cook over a medium heat for 2–3 minutes, stirring frequently, until golden brown. Remove the onion with a slotted spoon and drain well on absorbent kitchen paper. As they cool, they will turn crispy.

Pour the cooled soup into a food processor or blender and process to form a smooth purée. Return to the cleaned pan, adjust the seasoning, then stir in the cream. Gently reheat and top with the crispy onions. Serve immediately with chunks of crusty bread.

Cock-a-Leekie Soup

INGREDIENTS   SERVES 6

1 boiling fowl, about 1.8 kg/4 lb, including legs and wings

3 rashers streaky bacon, chopped

2.25 litres/4 pints chicken stock or water

450 g/1 lb leeks, cleaned and cut into 2.5 cm/1 inch pieces

1 bouquet garni (made up of a bay leaf, fresh parsley and thyme stalks, tied together in a bundle)

salt and freshly ground black pepper

25 g/1 oz pearl barley

125 g/4 oz ready-to-eat prunes, pitted (optional)

1 tsp soft brown sugar

freshly chopped flat-leaf parsley, to serve

FOOD FACT

This traditional Scottish dish is sometimes called 'Auld Reekie' Cock-a-Leekie, which refers to the recipe's origins in Edinburgh. It is often served at Burns Suppers or St Andrew's Night dinners.

Put the boiling fowl and bacon in a large saucepan and cover with the stock or water. Bring to the boil and use a slotted spoon to remove any scum as it rises to the surface.

Add three-quarters of the leeks (green as well as white sections) and the bouquet garni. Season with salt and pepper and return to the boil. Reduce the heat slightly and simmer gently for 2–3 hours, adding more water if necessary.

Remove the boiling fowl and leave until cool enough to handle. Add the pearl barley to the pan.

While the pearl parley is cooking for 15 minutes, return your attention to the fowl – you can either use this for another course or to make stock, or strip off the meat, discarding any skin, cut the meat into small pieces and return to the soup (it should have some pieces of chicken in it when served).

Add the prunes (if using) and remaining leeks and simmer for another 30 minutes. Check the seasoning and add the sugar if needed. Serve hot with a little chopped parsley sprinkled over the top.

Scotch Broth

INGREDIENTS   **SERVES 4**

Trim off any excess fat from the mutton and prepare the meat by wiping it with a damp cloth.

Put the mutton, barley and dried peas in a large saucepan with 2.75 litres/5 pints water. Bring to the boil and skim off any excess fat that rises to the surface. Reduce the heat slightly, season with salt and black pepper, and simmer gently for about 1 hour.

Add the carrots, turnips, onion and leek to the saucepan. Return to the boil, then reduce the heat slightly once again and simmer for 20 minutes, or until the vegetables are just cooked. Tip in the cabbage and check the seasoning. Simmer for another 15 minutes.

Remove the mutton from the saucepan, cut the meat into small pieces and discard the bone. Return the mutton to the pan.

A few minutes before serving, sprinkle in the parsley. Serve the broth piping hot.

900 g/2 lb mutton

75 g/3 oz pearl barley

75 g/3 oz dried peas

salt and freshly ground black pepper

3 carrots, diced

2 white turnips, diced

1 large onion, diced

1 large leek, white parts only, diced

1 small cabbage, shredded

2 tbsp chopped flat-leaf parsley

FOOD FACT

Traditionally, when this soup was made, the mutton would often be served as a main course rather than being diced and returned to the saucepan. It remains a popular dish and is often served on New Year's Day.

Partan Bree

INGREDIENTS   **SERVES 4**

50 g/2 oz long-grain white rice

600 ml/1 pint milk

600 ml/1 pint fish stock or liquor from boiling the crab

1 large cooked crab

125 ml/4 fl oz single cream

salt and freshly ground black pepper

fresh chives or parsley, finely chopped

Put the rice in a pan with the milk and stock or cooking liquor, bring to the boil and simmer until tender.

Meanwhile, remove all the meat from the crab, keeping the white claw meat separate.

Put the rice, liquid and brown crab meat in a blender or food processor and liquidise. Rinse the pan. Return the mixture to the pan, add the white meat and cream and reheat. Add salt and pepper to taste. If the partan bree is too thick, you can add some more milk.

Serve garnished with the chives or parsley.

Arbroath Toasties

INGREDIENTS   SERVES 4

Heat the smoked haddock in 150 ml/¼ pint of the milk in a saucepan. Bring to the boil, reduce the heat, cover and cook for 5 minutes, or until the fish flakes easily with a fork. Remove the fish with a fish slice and flake.

Mix the flour with the rest of the milk and then stir into the milk in the saucepan. Bring to the boil and cook for two minutes, stirring continuously until thick.

Stir in the cheese, egg yolk and flaked fish. Season to taste with salt and freshly ground black pepper, then heat through.

Whisk the egg white until it is stiff and fold into the fish mixture with a metal spoon.

Put the toast on a grill rack and spoon a quarter of the fish mixture onto each slice of toast. Place under a hot grill until the topping is lightly browned and serve immediately.

Ingredients
175 g/6 oz smoked haddock
175 ml/6 fl oz milk
2 tbsp plain flour
25 g/1 oz strong, hard, grated cheese
1 egg, separated into white and yolk
salt and freshly ground black pepper
4 slices buttered toast

Potato Pancakes with Smoked Salmon

INGREDIENTS   SERVES 4

450 g/1 lb floury potatoes, peeled and quartered

salt and freshly ground black pepper

1 large egg

1 large egg yolk

25 g/1 oz butter

25 g/1 oz plain flour

150 ml/¼ pint double cream

2 tbsp freshly chopped parsley

5 tbsp crème fraîche

1 tbsp horseradish sauce

225 g/8 oz smoked salmon, sliced

salad leaves, to serve

To garnish:

lemon slices

snipped chives

HELPFUL HINT

Commercially-made horseradish sauces vary in hotness, so it is best to add a little at a time to the crème fraîche and taste until you have the desired flavour.

Cook the potatoes in a sauce-pan of lightly salted boiling water for 15–20 minutes until tender. Drain thoroughly, then mash until free of lumps. Beat in the whole egg and egg yolk, together with the butter. Beat until smooth and creamy. Slowly beat in the flour and cream, then season to taste with salt and pepper. Stir in the chopped parsley.

Beat the crème fraîche and horseradish sauce together in a small bowl, cover with cling-film and reserve.

Heat a lightly oiled, heavy-based frying pan over a medium-high heat. Place a few spoonfuls of the potato mixture in the hot pan and cook for 4–5 minutes until cooked and golden, turning halfway through cooking time. Remove from the pan, drain on absorbent kitchen paper and keep warm. Repeat with the remaining mixture.

Arrange the pancakes on individual serving plates. Place the smoked salmon on the pancakes and spoon over a little of the horseradish sauce. Serve with salad and the remaining horseradish sauce and garnish with lemon slices and chives.

Creamy Salmon with Dill in Filo Baskets

INGREDIENTS   **SERVES 4**

Preheat the oven to 200°C/400°F/Gas Mark 6. Place the bay leaf, peppercorns, parsley and salmon in a frying pan and add enough water to barely cover the fish.

Bring to the boil, reduce the heat and poach the fish for 5 minutes until it flakes easily. Remove it from the pan. Reserve.

Spray each sheet of filo pastry lightly with the oil. Scrunch up the pastry to make a nest shape approximately 12.5 cm/5 inches in diameter. Place on a lightly oiled baking sheet and cook in the preheated oven for 10 minutes until golden and crisp.

Blanch the spinach in a pan of lightly salted boiling water for 2 minutes. Drain thoroughly and keep warm.

Mix the fromage frais, mustard and dill together, then warm gently. Season to taste with salt and pepper. Divide the spinach between the filo pastry nests and flake the salmon onto the spinach.

Spoon the mustard and dill sauce over the filo baskets and serve immediately.

Ingredients
1 bay leaf
6 black peppercorns
1 large fresh parsley sprig
175 g/6 oz salmon fillet
4 large sheets filo pastry
fine spray of oil
125 g/4 oz baby spinach leaves
8 tbsp low-fat fromage frais
2 tsp Dijon mustard
2 tbsp freshly chopped dill
salt and freshly ground black pepper

FOOD FACT

This is a highly nutritious dish, combining calcium-rich salmon with vitamin- and mineral-rich spinach. The low-fat fromage frais in this recipe can be substituted with low-fat live yogurt if you want to aid digestion and give the immune system a real boost!

Pumpkin & Smoked Haddock Soup

INGREDIENTS   SERVES 4–6

2 tbsp olive oil

1 medium onion, peeled and chopped

2 garlic cloves, peeled and chopped

3 celery stalks, trimmed and chopped

700 g/1½ lb pumpkin, peeled, deseeded and cut into chunks

450 g/1 lb potatoes, peeled and cut into chunks

750 ml/1¼ pints chicken stock, heated

125 ml/4 fl oz dry sherry

200 g/7 oz smoked haddock fillet

150 ml/¼ pint milk

freshly ground black pepper

2 tbsp freshly chopped parsley

FOOD FACT

Try to find undyed smoked haddock for this soup rather than the brightly coloured yellow type, as the texture and flavour is better.

Heat the oil in a large heavy-based saucepan and gently cook the onion, garlic and celery for about 10 minutes. This will release the sweetness but not colour the vegetables. Add the pumpkin and potatoes to the saucepan and stir to coat the vegetables with the oil.

Gradually pour in the stock and bring to the boil. Cover, then reduce the heat and simmer for 25 minutes, stirring occasionally. Stir in the dry sherry, then remove the saucepan from the heat and leave to cool for 5–10 minutes.

Blend the mixture in a food processor or blender to form a chunky purée and return to the cleaned saucepan.

Meanwhile, place the fish in a shallow frying pan. Pour in the milk with 3 tablespoons of water and bring to almost boiling point. Reduce the heat, cover and simmer for 6 minutes, or until the fish is cooked and flakes easily. Remove from the heat and, using a slotted spoon, remove the fish from the liquid, reserving both liquid and fish.

Discard the skin and any bones from the fish and flake into pieces. Stir the fish liquid into the soup, together with the flaked fish. Season with freshly ground black pepper, stir in the parsley and serve immediately.

Finnan Haddie Tart

INGREDIENTS **SERVES 6**

Preheat the oven to 190°C/375°F/Gas Mark 5. Sift the flour and salt into a large bowl. Add the fats and mix lightly. Using your fingertips, rub into the flour until the mixture resembles breadcrumbs.

Sprinkle 1 tablespoon cold water into the mixture and, with a knife, start bringing the dough together. It may be necessary to use the hands for the final stage. If the dough does not form a ball instantly, add a little more water. Put the pastry in a polythene bag and chill for at least 30 minutes.

On a lightly floured surface, roll out the pastry and use to line an 18 cm/7 inch lightly oiled quiche or flan tin. Prick the base all over with a fork and bake blind in the preheated oven for 15 minutes.

Carefully remove the pastry from the oven and brush with a little of the beaten egg. Return to the oven for a further 5 minutes, then place the fish in the pastry case.

For the filling, beat together the eggs and cream. Add the mustard, black pepper and cheese and pour over the fish. Sprinkle with the chives and bake for 35–40 minutes until the filling is golden brown and set in the centre. Serve hot or cold with the lemon and tomato wedges and salad leaves.

For the shortcrust pastry:

150 g/5 oz plain flour

pinch salt

25 g/1 oz lard or white vegetable fat, cut into small cubes

40 g/1½ oz butter or hard margarine, cut into small cubes

For the filling:

225 g/8 oz smoked haddock, skinned and cubed

2 large eggs, beaten

300 ml/½ pint double cream

1 tsp Dijon mustard

freshly ground black pepper

125 g/4 oz Gruyère cheese, grated

1 tbsp freshly snipped chives

To serve:

lemon wedges

tomato wedges

fresh green salad leaves

FOOD FACT

In the late nineteenth century, as fast transportation by train became available, the Aberdeen fishing village of Findon (pronounced locally as 'Finnan') began producing lightly smoked and delicately flavoured haddock (haddies) which were of a much finer texture than anything available up until then. They were an immediate success and have been used in many different recipes ever since.

Cullen Skink

INGREDIENTS   SERVES 4

25 g/1 oz unsalted butter

1 onion, peeled and chopped

1 fresh bay leaf

25 g/1 oz plain flour

350 g/12 oz new potatoes, scrubbed and cut into small pieces

600 ml/1 pint semi-skimmed milk

300 ml/½ pint water

350 g/12 oz undyed smoked haddock fillet, skinned

75 g/3 oz sweetcorn kernels

50 g/2 oz garden peas

freshly ground black pepper

½ tsp freshly grated nutmeg

2–3 tbsp single cream

2 tbsp freshly chopped parsley

crusty bread, to serve

Melt the butter in a large heavy-based saucepan, add the onion and sauté for 3 minutes, stirring occasionally. Add the bay leaf and stir, then sprinkle in the flour and cook over a low heat for 2 minutes, stirring frequently. Add the potatoes.

Take off the heat and gradually stir in the milk and water. Return to the heat and bring to the boil, stirring. Reduce the heat to a simmer and cook for 10 minutes.

Meanwhile, discard any pin bones from the fish and cut into small pieces. Add to the pan together with the sweetcorn and peas. Cover and cook gently, stirring occasionally, for 10 minutes, or until the vegetables and fish are cooked.

Add pepper and nutmeg to taste, then stir in the cream and heat gently for 1–2 minutes, or until piping hot. Sprinkle with the parsley and serve with crusty bread.

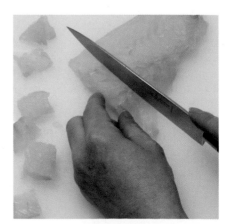

Potato Pancakes & Mackerel

INGREDIENTS MAKES 6 PANCAKES

To make the sauce, mix together the crème fraîche, horseradish, lime zest and juice and chives. Cover and reserve.

To make the pancakes, place the potatoes in a large saucepan and cover with lightly salted boiling water. Bring back to the boil, cover and simmer for 15 minutes, or until the potatoes are tender. Drain and mash until smooth. Cool for 5 minutes, then whisk in the egg white, milk, flour, thyme and salt to form a thick smooth batter. Leave to stand for 30 minutes, then stir before using.

Heat a little oil in a heavy-based frying pan. Add 2–3 large spoonfuls of batter to make a small pancake and cook for 1–2 minutes until golden. Flip the pancake and cook for a further minute, or until golden. Repeat with the remaining batter to make 8 pancakes.

Arrange the pancakes on a plate and top with the smoked mackerel. Garnish with herbs and serve immediately with spoonfuls of the reserved horseradish sauce.

For the sauce:

4 tbsp crème fraîche

1 tbsp horseradish sauce

grated zest and juice of 1 lime

1 tbsp freshly snipped chives

For the pancakes:

225 g/8 oz floury potatoes, peeled and cut into chunks

1 small egg white

2 tbsp milk

2 tsp self-raising flour

1 tbsp freshly chopped thyme

large pinch salt

a little vegetable oil, for frying

225 g/8 oz smoked mackerel fillets, skinned and roughly chopped

fresh herbs, to garnish

HELPFUL HINT

Keep the pancakes warm as you make them by stacking on a warmed plate. Place greaseproof paper between each pancake to keep them separate and fold a clean tea towel loosely over the top. If preferred, the pancakes can be made in advance and frozen, interleaved with nonstick baking parchment. To serve, thaw, then reheat the stack of pancakes, covered in kitchen foil, in a moderate oven.

Smoked Mackerel Vol-au-Vents

INGREDIENTS **SERVES 1–2**

350 g/12 oz prepared puff pastry

1 small egg, beaten

2 tsp sesame seeds

225 g/8 oz peppered smoked mackerel, skinned and chopped

5 cm/2 inch piece cucumber

4 tbsp soft cream cheese

2 tbsp cranberry sauce

1 tbsp freshly chopped dill

1 tbsp finely grated lemon zest

dill sprigs, to garnish

mixed salad leaves, to serve

Preheat the oven to 230°C/450°F/Gas Mark 8. Roll the pastry out on a lightly floured surface and, using a 9 cm/3½ inch fluted cutter, cut out 12 rounds. Using a 1 cm/½ inch cutter, mark a lid in the centre of each round. Place on a damp baking sheet and brush the rounds with a little beaten egg.

Sprinkle the pastry with the sesame seeds and bake in the preheated oven for 10–12 minutes, or until golden brown and well risen.

Transfer the vol-au-vents to a chopping board and, when cool enough to touch, carefully remove the lids with a small sharp knife. Scoop out any uncooked pastry from the inside of each vol-au-vent, then return to the oven for 5–8 minutes to dry out. Remove and allow to cool.

Flake the mackerel into small pieces and reserve. Peel the cucumber if desired, cut into very small dice and add to the mackerel.

Beat the soft cream cheese with the cranberry sauce, dill and lemon zest. Stir in the mackerel and cucumber and use to fill the vol-au-vents. Place the lids on top and garnish with dill sprigs. Serve with mmixed salad leaves.

MEAT & POULTRY

Shepherd's Pie

INGREDIENTS   SERVES 4

2 tbsp vegetable or olive oil

1 onion, peeled and finely chopped

1 carrot, peeled and finely chopped

1 celery stalk, trimmed and finely chopped

1 tbsp fresh thyme sprigs

450 g/1 lb leftover roast lamb,
finely chopped

150 ml/¼ pint red wine

150 ml/¼ pint lamb or vegetable stock
or leftover gravy

2 tbsp tomato purée

salt and freshly ground black pepper

700 g/1½ lb potatoes, peeled and
cut into chunks

25 g/1 oz butter

6 tbsp milk

1 tbsp freshly chopped parsley

fresh herbs, to garnish

HELPFUL HINT

A traditional Shepherd's Pie is always
made from cold roast lamb, but you
can make it with fresh minced lamb
if preferred. Simply dry-fry 450 g/1 lb
lean mince in a nonstick frying pan
over a high heat until well browned,
then follow the recipe as before.

Preheat the oven to 200°C/400°F/Gas Mark 6, about 15 minutes before cooking. Heat the oil in a large saucepan and add the onion, carrot and celery. Cook over a medium heat for 8–10 minutes until softened and starting to brown.

Add the thyme and cook briefly, then add the cooked lamb, wine, stock and tomato purée. Season to taste with salt and pepper and simmer gently for 25–30 minutes until reduced and thickened. Remove from the heat to cool slightly and season again.

Meanwhile, boil the potatoes in plenty of salted water for 12–15 minutes until tender. Drain and return to the saucepan over a low heat to dry out. Remove from the heat and add the butter, milk and parsley. Mash until creamy, adding a little more milk if necessary. Adjust the seasoning.

Transfer the lamb mixture to a shallow ovenproof dish. Spoon the mash over the filling and spread evenly to cover completely. Fork the surface, place on a baking sheet, then cook in the preheated oven for 25–30 minutes until the potato topping is browned and the filling is piping hot. Garnish and serve.

Haggis

INGREDIENTS   SERVES 4

set of sheep's heart, lungs and liver, cleaned by a butcher

350 g/12 oz finely chopped suet

125 g/4 oz medium ground oatmeal

2 medium onions, finely chopped

125 ml/4 fl oz beef stock

1 tsp salt

½ tsp black pepper

1 tsp nutmeg

½ tsp mace

one beef bung (intestine)

FOOD FACT

Haggis must be the most famous Scottish dish of all. It owes its world renowned status in no small part to Robert Burn's poem 'Address to a Haggis' of 1878 and is most commonly consumed on Burns night alongside mashed 'neeps and tatties'.

Trim off any excess fat and sinew from the sheep's organs and, if present, discard the windpipe. Place in a large pan, cover with water and bring to the boil. Reduce the heat and simmer for an hour or possibly longer to ensure that they are all tender. Drain and cool.

Finely chop the meat and combine in a large bowl with the suet, oatmeal, finely chopped onions, beef stock, salt, pepper, nutmeg and mace. Make sure the ingredients are well mixed. Stuff the meat mixture into the beef bung, which should be over half full. Then press out the air and tie the open ends tightly with string. Make sure that you leave room for the mixture to expand, or it may burst while cooking. If it looks as though it may do that, prick with a sharp needle to reduce the pressure.

Place in a pot and cover with water. Bring to the boil and immediately reduce the heat and simmer, covered, for three hours. Avoid boiling vigorously or you may burst the skin.

Serve hot with 'champit tatties and bashit neeps' (mashed potato and turnip or swede). For added flavour, you can add some nutmeg to the potatoes and allspice to the turnip or swede.

Steak Balmoral

INGREDIENTS   **SERVES 4**

Heat a little oil or butter in a large frying pan. Pan-fry the steaks to taste, working in batches if necessary, remove from the pan and keep warm.

Melt the butter in the pan and fry the shallot until soft. Add the whisky to the pan and carefully set it alight. Add the cream, stock, mushrooms and mustard and bring to the boil. Simmer gently until the sauce has reduced by half, stirring from time to time. Season to taste with salt and pepper.

Put the steaks on individual serving plates and pour over the sauce. Serve immediately.

---

vegetable oil or butter, for frying

4 Aberdeen Angus steaks

25 g/1 oz butter

1 shallot, chopped

4 tbsp Scotch whisky

300 ml/½ pint double cream

150 ml/¼ pint beef stock

125 g/4 oz mushrooms, sliced

1 tsp coarse-grain mustard

salt and freshly ground black pepper, to taste

Forfar Bridies

INGREDIENTS   **MAKES 6**

If using rump steak, remove any fat or gristle from the meat and beat with a meat bat or rolling pin. Cut into 1 cm/½ inch pieces and place in a medium-sized bowl. Add the suet, or butter or margarine, together with the chopped onion, mustard powder, beef stock and salt and pepper and mix well.

Prepare the pastry and divide the pastry and meat mixture into six equal portions. Roll each pastry portion into a circle about 15 cm/6 inches in diameter and about 5 mm/¼ inch thick and place a portion of the mixture in the centre. Leave an edge of pastry showing all round.

Brush the outer edge of half the pastry circle with water and fold over. Crimp the edges together well. The crimped edges should be at the top of each bridie. Make a small slit in the top to let out any steam.

Brush a baking tray with oil and place the bridies on this, ensuring that they are not touching. Place in a preheated oven at 230°C/450°F/Gas Mark 8 for 15 minutes, then reduce the temperature to 180°C/350°F/Gas Mark 4 and cook for another 45–55 minutes. They should be golden brown – if they are getting too dark, cover with greaseproof paper. Serve immediately.

---

700 g/1½ lb boneless lean rump steak or lean minced beef

50 g/2 oz suet or butter or margarine

1 onion, finely chopped

1 tsp dry mustard powder

50 ml/2 fl oz rich beef stock

salt and freshly ground black pepper, to taste

700 g/1½ lb ready-made flaky pastry

HELPFUL HINT

The original recipe for Forfar Bridies uses suet, but as this is not to everyone's taste, it can be substituted with butter or margarine.

Scotch Pie

INGREDIENTS   MAKES 8–10 PIES

For the meat filling:

450 g/1 lb lean lamb, minced

pinch mace or nutmeg

salt and freshly ground black pepper

150 ml/¼ pint gravy

For the hot water pastry:

450 g/1 lb plain flour

pinch salt

175 g/6 oz lard

200 ml/7 fl oz water, approximately

milk, for glazing

You will also need:

glasses or jars, approximately 7.5–8.5 cm/
3–3½ inches in diameter, to shape the pies

HELPFUL HINT

If the pies are not eaten immediately,
they can be stored in the refrigerator.
Always ensure that they are properly
reheated before being eaten.

To make the meat filling, mix the minced lamb, spice and seasoning together in a bowl. Put this to one side while you make the pastry.

To make the pastry, sift the flour and salt into a warm bowl, making a well in the centre of the flour. Melt the lard in a small measure of water and, when it is bubbling, add to the flour and mix thoroughly.

Take a small amount of pastry (remember the mixture should make 8–10 pies, with their tops) and form into a ball. Keep the rest of the pastry warm while making each pastry case. Roll the pastry out and shape it around the base of a glass or jar approximately 7.5–8.5 cm/3–3½ inches in diameter. Make sure there are no cracks in the pastry. Trim round the top to make it even. As the pastry cools, remove the glass and continue until you have about a quarter of the pastry left to make the lids.

Fill the cases with the meat and add the gravy to keep the meat moist. Roll out the remaining pastry and use the glass or jar to cut the lids to size. Wet the edges of the lids, place over the meat and press down lightly over the filling. Pinch the edges and trim. Cut a small hole or vent in the centre of each lid to allow any steam to escape. Glaze with milk and bake for about 45 minutes at 140°C/275°F/Gas Mark 1. Serve.

Braised Lamb with Broad Beans

INGREDIENTS   SERVES 4

Trim the lamb, discarding any fat or gristle, then place the flour in a polythene bag, add the lamb and toss until coated thoroughly. Peel and slice the onion and garlic and reserve. Heat the olive oil in a heavy-based saucepan and, when hot, add the lamb and cook, stirring, until the meat is sealed and browned all over. Using a slotted spoon, transfer the lamb to a plate and reserve.

Add the onion and garlic to the saucepan and cook for 3 minutes, stirring frequently, until softened, then return the lamb to the saucepan. Add the chopped tomatoes with their juice, the stock, the chopped thyme and oregano to the pan and season to taste with salt and pepper. Bring to the boil, then cover with a close-fitting lid, reduce the heat and simmer for 1 hour.

Add the broad beans to the lamb and simmer for 20–30 minutes, or until the lamb is tender. Garnish with fresh oregano and serve with creamy mashed potatoes.

700 g/1½ lb lamb, cut into large chunks

1 tbsp plain flour

1 onion

2 garlic cloves

1 tbsp olive oil

400 g can chopped tomatoes with basil

300 ml/½ pint lamb stock

2 tbsp freshly chopped thyme

2 tbsp freshly chopped oregano

salt and freshly ground black pepper

150 g/5 oz frozen broad beans

fresh oregano, to garnish

creamy mashed potatoes, to serve

TASTY TIP

If you want to use fresh broad beans in season, you will need about 450 g/1 lb of beans in their pods for this recipe. If you prefer to peel the beans, plunge them first into boiling salted water for about 30 seconds, drain and refresh under cold water. The skins will come off very easily.

Pan-fried Beef with Creamy Mushrooms

INGREDIENTS · SERVES 4

Cut the shallots in half if large, then chop the garlic. Heat the oil in a large frying pan and cook the shallots for about 8 minutes, stirring occasionally, until almost softened. Add the garlic and beef and cook for 8–10 minutes, turning once during cooking until the meat is browned all over. Using a slotted spoon, transfer the beef to a plate and keep warm.

Rinse the tomatoes and cut into eighths, then wipe and slice the mushrooms. Add to the pan and cook for 5 minutes, stirring frequently, until the mushrooms have softened.

Pour in the brandy and heat through. Draw the pan off the heat and carefully ignite. Allow the flames to subside. Pour in the wine, return to the heat and bring to the boil. Boil until reduced by one third. Draw the pan off the heat, season to taste with salt and pepper, add the cream and stir.

Arrange the beef on serving plates and spoon over the sauce. Serve with baby new potatoes and a few green beans.

225 g/8 oz shallots, peeled

2 garlic cloves, peeled

2 tbsp olive oil

4 beef medallions

4 plum tomatoes

125 g/4 oz flat mushrooms

3 tbsp brandy

150 ml/¼ pint red wine

salt and freshly ground black pepper

4 tbsp double cream

To serve:

baby new potatoes

freshly cooked green beans

HELPFUL HINT

To prepare medallions of beef, buy a piece of fillet weighing approximately 700 g/1½ lb. Cut crossways into 4 pieces.

Beef & Red Wine Pie

INGREDIENTS   **SERVES 4**

700 g/1½ lb stewing beef, cubed

4 tbsp seasoned plain flour

2 tbsp sunflower oil

2 onions, peeled and chopped

2 garlic cloves, peeled and crushed

1 tbsp freshly chopped thyme

300 ml/½ pint red wine

150 ml/¼ pint beef stock

1–2 tsp Worcestershire sauce

2 tbsp tomato ketchup

2 bay leaves

knob butter

225 g/8 oz button mushrooms

225 g/8 oz ready-made flaky pastry, chilled

beaten egg or milk, to glaze

parsley sprig, to garnish

HELPFUL HINT

Shortcrust or puff pastry could also be used to top the pie in this recipe. It is important, though, whichever pastry is used, to brush the pie with beaten egg or milk before baking, as this will result in an appetising golden crust.

Preheat the oven to 200°C/400°F/Gas Mark 6. Toss the beef cubes in the seasoned flour.

Heat the oil in a large heavy-based frying pan. Fry the beef in batches for about 5 minutes until golden brown. Return all of the beef to the pan and add the onions, garlic and thyme. Fry for about 10 minutes, stirring occasionally. If the beef begins to stick, add a little water.

Add the red wine and stock and bring to the boil. Stir in the Worcestershire sauce, tomato ketchup and bay leaves. Cover and simmer on a very low heat for about 1 hour until the beef is tender.

Heat the butter and gently sauté the mushrooms until golden brown. Add to the stew. Simmer uncovered for a further 15 minutes. Remove the bay leaves. Spoon the beef into a 1.1 litre/2 pint pie dish and reserve.

Roll out the pastry on a lightly floured surface. Cut out the lid to 5 mm/¼ inch wider than the dish. Brush the rim with the beaten egg and lay the pastry lid on top. Press to seal, then knock the edges with the back of the knife.

Cut a slit in the lid and brush with the beaten egg or milk to glaze. Bake in the preheated oven for 30 minutes, or until golden brown. Garnish with the parsley sprig and serve immediately.

Steak & Kidney Stew

Heat the oil in a large heavy-based saucepan, add the onion, garlic and celery and sauté for 5 minutes, or until browned. Remove from the pan with a slotted spoon and reserve.

Add the steak and kidneys to the pan and cook for 3–5 minutes, or until sealed, then return the onion mixture to the pan. Sprinkle in the flour and cook, stirring, for 2 minutes. Take off the heat, stir in the tomato purée, then the stock and season to taste with salt and pepper. Add the bay leaf.

Return to the heat and bring to the boil, stirring occasionally. Add the carrots, then reduce the heat to a simmer and cover with a lid. Cook for 1¼ hours, stirring occasionally. Reduce the heat if the liquid is evaporating quickly. Add the potatoes and cook for a further 30 minutes.

Place the flour, suet and herbs in a bowl and add a little seasoning. Add the water and mix to a stiff mixture. Using a little extra flour, shape into 8 small balls. Place the dumplings on top of the stew, cover with the lid and continue to cook for 15 minutes, or until the meat is tender and the dumplings are well risen and fluffy. Stir in the spinach and leave to stand for 2 minutes, or until the spinach has wilted.

INGREDIENTS　　　SERVES 4

| 1 tbsp olive oil |
| 1 onion, peeled and chopped |
| 2–3 garlic cloves, peeled and crushed |
| 2 celery stalks, trimmed and sliced |
| 550 g/1¼ lb braising steak, trimmed and diced |
| 125 g/4 oz lambs' kidneys, cored and chopped |
| 2 tbsp plain flour |
| 1 tbsp tomato purée |
| 900 ml/1½ pints beef stock |
| salt and freshly ground black pepper |
| 1 fresh bay leaf |
| 300 g/10 oz carrots, peeled and sliced |
| 350 g/12 oz baby new potatoes, scrubbed |
| 350 g/12 oz fresh spinach leaves, chopped |

For the dumplings:

| 125 g/4 oz self-raising flour |
| 50 g/2 oz shredded suet |
| 1 tbsp freshly chopped mixed herbs |
| 2–3 tbsp water |

Seared Calves' Liver with Onions & Mustard Mash

INGREDIENTS   SERVES 2

2 tbsp olive oil

100 g/3½ oz butter

3 large onions, peeled and finely sliced

pinch sugar

salt and freshly ground black pepper

1 tbsp fresh thyme sprigs

1 tbsp balsamic vinegar

700 g/1½ lb potatoes, peeled and
cut into chunks

6–8 tbsp milk

1–2 tsp, or to taste, wholegrain mustard

3–4 fresh sage leaves

550 g/1¼ lb thinly sliced calves' liver

1 tsp lemon juice

HELPFUL HINT

Calves' liver is mild and tender and needs only brief cooking over a high heat to sear the outside, but keep it moist and juicy within. Lambs' liver may be used for this recipe instead, but tone down the slightly stronger flavour by soaking in milk for up to 1 hour before cooking.

Preheat the oven to 150°C/300°F/Gas Mark 2. Heat half the oil and 25 g/1 oz of the butter in a flameproof casserole. When foaming, add the onions. Cover and cook over a low heat for 20 minutes until softened and beginning to collapse. Add the sugar and season with salt and pepper. Stir in the thyme. Cover the casserole and transfer to the preheated oven. Cook for a further 30–45 minutes until softened completely but not browned. Remove from the oven and stir in the balsamic vinegar.

Meanwhile, boil the potatoes in boiling salted water for 15–18 minutes until tender. Drain well, then return to the pan. Place over a low heat to dry completely, remove from the heat and stir in 50 g/2 oz of the butter, the milk, mustard and salt and pepper to taste. Mash thoroughly until creamy and keep warm.

Heat a large frying pan and add the remaining butter and oil. When it is foaming, add the sage leaves and stir for a few seconds, then add the liver. Cook over a high heat for 1–2 minutes on each side. It should remain slightly pink: do not overcook. Remove the liver from the pan. Add the lemon juice to the pan and swirl around to deglaze.

To serve, place a large spoonful of the mashed potato on each plate. Top with some of the melting onions, the liver and finally the pan juices.

Roasted Grouse with Black Pudding

INGREDIENTS   SERVES 4

500 g/1 lb 2 oz

new potatoes

4 celery stalks

1 leek

2 small courgettes

12 baby asparagus tips

8 baby onions

3 tbsp olive oil

50 g/2 oz butter

salt and pepper to taste

4 whole grouse, oven-ready

4 oz shallots

2 fresh thyme stalks, chopped

25 ml/1 fl oz Madeira

300 ml/½ pint game or beef gravy

4 slices black pudding

Place the new potatoes in a pan, cover with salted water and par-boil for 10–12 minutes. Drain and refresh under cold water until cool. While the potatoes are cooking, wash, trim and cut the celery, leek and courgettes crossways into 2 cm/¾ inch rounds at an angle. Leave the asparagus and onions whole. Lightly season the vegetables and brush with olive oil.

Preheat a griddle pan. Slice the new potatoes lengthways into quarters and fry them with the vegetables on the griddle to create a crisscross effect. Remove and place on an oven tray to reheat later.

Preheat the oven to 200°C/400°F/Gas Mark 6. Heat the remaining olive oil and 25 g/1 oz of the butter in a heavy-based frying pan. Season the grouse, place in the pan and seal on all sides. Place in a roasting tray and cook in the oven for about 20 minutes. Leave to rest for approximately 5 minutes.

To make the sauce, peel and finely shred the shallots. Melt the remaining butter in a saucepan, add the shallots and thyme and cover. Cook for about 2 minutes until just transparent. Add the Madeira and the game or beef gravy and bring to the boil. Strain and set aside.

Grill the black pudding on both sides until cooked and crispy. Place on kitchen paper to drain for a few seconds. While the black pudding is cooking, place the vegetables back into the oven for 2–3 minutes to reheat. Place a grouse, a slice of black pudding and some vegetables on each plate, spoon the sauce over and serve.

Chicken Bonnie Prince Charlie

INGREDIENTS　　　　**SERVES 4**

Mix the flour with the salt and pepper in a large dish and use to flour and season the chicken fillets.

Melt the butter in a large frying pan and fry the chicken on both sides. When they are well browned, sprinkle with Drambuie, add the chicken stock, then cover and simmer for ten minutes.

While the chicken is cooking, peel and core the apples and cut them into thick slices. Melt the butter in a pan and cook the apples gently until fairly soft – do not stir, to avoid mashing. Remove the chicken to a serving dish when ready and keep warm in the oven.

Make the sauce by adding more Drambuie, if required, to the stock left in the pan and gently stir in the cream. Heat but do not boil, then add the roasted flaked almonds.

Cover the chicken with the sauce and garnish with the sliced apple. Serve immediately.

Ingredients
a little flour
salt and freshly ground black pepper
4 skinless chicken breast fillets
25 g/1 oz butter, for frying
2–3 tbsp Drambuie
125 ml/4 fl oz chicken stock
4 apples
75 g/3 oz butter
250 ml/8 fl oz double cream
25 g/1 oz roasted flaked almonds

FOOD FACT

Drambuie is a liqueur that combines fine Scotch whiskies with heather honey and other secret ingredients. The recipe for the liqueur is said to have been given to the MacKinnon clan by Bonnie Prince Charlie in gratitude for their help after the Battle of Culloden in 1746.

Braised Chicken in Beer

INGREDIENTS   SERVES 4

4 chicken joints, skinned

125 g/4 oz pitted dried prunes

2 bay leaves

12 shallots

2 tsp olive oil

125 g/4 oz small button mushrooms, wiped

1 tsp soft dark brown sugar

½ tsp wholegrain mustard

2 tsp tomato purée

150 ml/¼ pint light ale

150 ml/¼ pint chicken stock

salt and freshly ground black pepper

2 tsp cornflour

2 tsp lemon juice

2 tbsp chopped fresh parsley

flat-leaf parsley, to garnish

To serve:

mashed potatoes

seasonal green vegetables

Preheat the oven to 170°C/325°F/Gas Mark 3. Cut each chicken joint in half and put in an ovenproof casserole with the prunes and bay leaves.

To peel the shallots, put in a small bowl and cover with boiling water. Drain them after 2 minutes and rinse under cold water until cool enough to handle. The skins should then peel away easily from the shallots.

Heat the oil in a large nonstick frying pan. Add the shallots and cook gently for about 5 minutes until beginning to colour. Add the mushrooms to the pan and cook for a further 3–4 minutes until both the mushrooms and onions are softened.

Sprinkle the sugar over the shallots and mushrooms, then add the mustard, tomato purée, ale and chicken stock. Season to taste with salt and pepper and bring to the boil, stirring to combine. Carefully pour over the chicken. Cover the casserole and cook in the preheated oven for 1 hour.

Blend the cornflour with the lemon juice and 1 tablespoon of cold water and stir into the chicken casserole. Return the casserole to the oven for a further 10 minutes, or until the chicken is cooked and the vegetables are tender.

Remove the bay leaves and stir in the chopped parsley. Garnish the chicken with the flat-leaf parsley. Serve with the mashed potatoes and fresh green vegetables.

FISH & SEAFOOD

Smoked Haddock Kedgeree

INGREDIENTS   **SERVES 4**

450 g/1 lb smoked haddock fillets

50 g/2 oz butter

1 onion, peeled and finely chopped

2 tsp mild curry powder

175 g/6 oz long-grain rice

450 ml/¾ pint fish or vegetable stock, heated

2 large eggs, hard-boiled and shelled

2 tbsp freshly chopped parsley

2 tbsp whipping cream (optional)

salt and freshly ground black pepper

pinch cayenne pepper

FOOD FACT

The word *Khichri* means a mixture or hotchpotch in Hindi. The British in India, some argue a Scottish regiment in particular, adapted this dish, which was originally made with an assortment of spices simmered with rice and lentils, and turned it into kedgeree, adding flakes of smoked fish and hard-boiled eggs.

Place the haddock in a shallow frying pan and cover with 300 ml/½ pint water. Simmer gently for 8–10 minutes, or until the fish is cooked. Drain, then remove all the skin and bones from the fish and flake into a dish. Keep warm.

Melt the butter in a saucepan and add the chopped onion and curry powder. Cook, stirring, for 3–4 minutes, or until the onion is soft, then stir in the rice. Cook for a further minute, stirring continuously, then stir in the hot stock.

Cover and simmer gently for 15 minutes, or until the rice has absorbed all the liquid. Cut the eggs into quarters or eighths and add half to the mixture with half the parsley.

Carefully fold the cooked fish in to the mixture and add the cream, if using. Season to taste with salt and pepper. Heat the kedgeree through briefly until piping hot.

Transfer the mixture to a large dish and garnish with the remaining quartered eggs and parsley and serve with a pinch of cayenne pepper. Serve immediately.

Smoked Haddock Mornay

INGREDIENTS **SERVES 2**

2 tsp butter

50 g/2 oz Cheddar cheese

50 g/2 oz double cream

225 g/8 oz good-quality smoked haddock

1 tsp crushed black peppercorns

pinch salt

freshly chopped parsley

To serve:

mashed or boiled potatoes

steamed green vegetables

Melt the butter in a pan over a medium heat. Add the cheese and cream. When the cheese has melted, add the smoked haddock and pepper and salt. Cook for about 4 minutes each side. Preheat the grill to high.

Move the haddock to an ovenproof dish and pour over the sauce. Cook under the grill until golden brown. Sprinkle with freshly chopped parsley and serve with mashed or boiled potatoes and green vegetables.

Tweed Kettle

INGREDIENTS **SERVES 4**

450 g/1 lb fresh salmon, preferably from the tail end

salt and freshly ground black pepper

pinch ground mace

150 ml/¼ pint dry white wine

2 chopped shallots, or 1 tbsp chopped chives

25 g/1 oz butter

125 g/4 oz chopped mushrooms

1 tbsp freshly chopped parsley

Put the fish in a pan, just covered with water, and bring to the boil. Simmer gently for 5 minutes.

Remove the fish from the pan (reserving the cooking liquor), then remove the skin and any bones and cut or pull the fish into small pieces.

Season with salt and pepper and the ground mace and put into a clean dish with 150 ml/¼ pint of the reserved cooking liquor.

Add the wine and the finely chopped shallots or chives. Cover the dish and simmer gently for about 20 minutes.

Melt the butter in a frying pan and soften the mushrooms in it. Drain and add to the salmon and heat together for another 5 minutes. Serve with chopped parsley.

FOOD FACT

Also known as Salmon Hash, this dish was particularly popular in Edinburgh in the nineteenth century. Cod or haddock can be used instead of salmon, if preferred.

Ham & Haddie Pie

Preheat the oven to 190°C/375°F/Gas Mark 5. Grease a medium-sized ovenproof dish. Melt the butter in a pan and fry the onion until it is soft. Add the chopped bacon and cook for another 2 or 3 minutes.

Arrange half the tomato slices in the dish and cover with the onion and bacon mixture. Put the haddock on top of this and top with the remaining tomato slices.   Pour on the water and sprinkle with the breadcrumbs and cheese. Cover with a lid or kitchen foil and cook for 20 minutes in the preheated oven. Remove the lid or foil and cook for a further 10 minutes until the topping has turned brown.

2 tsp butter, for frying

1 small onion, chopped

125 g/4 oz bacon, chopped

250 g/9 oz tomatoes, sliced

375 g/13 oz smoked haddock

2–3 tbsp water

65 g/2½ oz breadcrumbs

65 g/2½ oz Scottish Cheddar cheese (or similar), grated

Trout in Oatmeal

If not already skinned, remove the skin from the fish.

Cut each skinned fillet of trout into four equal-sized pieces. Brush each portion with milk and coat with the oatmeal.

Place the trout on a baking tray, cover with clingfilm and chill in the refrigerator for 20 minutes.

For the parsley butter, warm the butter slightly to soften it and mash with a fork. Add the lemon juice, chopped spring onion and peppercorns and mix well. Add the parsley and mix again.

Form the butter mixture into a log shape and cut into rounds. Chill in the refrigerator until needed.

Heat the sunflower oil in a nonstick frying pan and cook the trout on each side for 2 minutes, or until the oatmeal has become golden. Serve with the parsley butter on top and accompanied by some freshly cooked vegetables.

2 large trout

small quantity milk

50 g/2 oz fine oatmeal

1 tbsp sunflower oil

freshly cooked vegetables, to serve

For the parsley butter:

75 g/3 oz butter

3 tsp lemon juice

1 spring onion, finely chopped

¼ tsp cracked black peppercorns

1 tbsp fresh parsley, finely chopped

FOOD FACT

Rolling fish in oatmeal is a traditional Scottish cooking technique. You can do it with any fish, but trout, herring and salmon are particularly good when eaten in this way.

Salmon Fish Cakes

INGREDIENTS   SERVES 4

225 g/8 oz potatoes, peeled

450 g/1 lb salmon fillet, skinned

125 g/4 oz carrot, trimmed and peeled

2 tbsp grated lemon zest

2–3 tbsp freshly chopped coriander

1 medium egg yolk

salt and freshly ground black pepper

2 tbsp plain white flour

few fine sprays of oil

To serve:

prepared tomato sauce

tossed green salad

crusty bread

Cube the potatoes and cook in lightly salted boiling water for 15 minutes. Drain and mash the potatoes. Place in a mixing bowl and reserve.

Place the salmon in a food processor and blend to form a chunky purée. Add the purée to the potatoes and mix together.

Coarsely grate the carrot and add to the fish with the lemon zest and the coriander.

Add the egg yolk, season to taste with salt and pepper, then gently mix the ingredients together. With damp hands, form the mixture into 4 large fish cakes. Coat in the flour and place on a plate. Cover loosely and chill for at least 30 minutes.

When ready to cook, spray a griddle pan with a few fine sprays of oil and heat the pan. When hot, add the fish cakes and cook on both sides for 3–4 minutes until the fish is cooked. Add an extra spray of oil, if needed, during cooking.

When the fish cakes are cooked, serve immediately with the tomato sauce, green salad and crusty bread.

Salmon with Herbed Potatoes

INGREDIENTS   **SERVES 4**

Preheat the oven to 190°C/375°F/Gas Mark 5, about 10 minutes before required. Parboil the potatoes in lightly salted boiling water for 5–8 minutes until they are barely tender. Drain and reserve.

Cut out 4 pieces of baking parchment, measuring 20.5 cm/8 inches square, and place on the work surface. Arrange the parboiled potatoes on top. Wipe the salmon steaks and place on top of the potatoes.

Place the carrot strips in a bowl with the asparagus spears, sugar snaps and grated lemon zest and juice. Season to taste with salt and pepper. Toss lightly together.

Divide the vegetables evenly between the salmon. Dot the top of each parcel with butter and a parsley sprig.

To wrap a parcel, lift up 2 opposite sides of the paper and fold the edges together. Twist the paper at the other 2 ends to seal the parcel well. Repeat with the remaining parcels.

Place the parcels on a baking tray and bake in the preheated oven for 15 minutes. Place an unopened parcel on each plate and open just before eating.

Ingredients
450 g/1 lb baby new potatoes
4 salmon steaks, each weighing about 175 g/6 oz
1 carrot, peeled and cut into fine strips
175 g/6 oz asparagus spears, trimmed
175 g/6 oz sugar snap peas, trimmed
finely grated zest and juice of 1 lemon
salt and freshly ground black pepper
25 g/1 oz butter
4 large fresh parsley sprigs

HELPFUL HINT

Cooking fish *en papillote* is an excellent way of keeping in all the juices, flavour and aroma of the fish and vegetables. Your guests will also enjoy the anticipation of opening these surprise packages. Do let the parcels stand for a few minutes before serving, as the steam can be burning hot when opened.

Salmon Noisettes with Fruity Sauce

INGREDIENTS   **SERVES 4**

4 × 125 g/4 oz salmon steaks

grated zest and juice of 2 lemons

grated zest and juice of 1 lime

3 tbsp olive oil

1 tbsp clear honey

1 tbsp wholegrain mustard

coarse sea salt and freshly ground black pepper

1 tbsp groundnut oil

125 g/4 oz mixed salad leaves, washed

1 bunch watercress, washed and thick stalks removed

250 g/9 oz baby plum tomatoes, halved

HELPFUL HINT

When choosing salad leaves for this dish, look out for slightly bitter leaves such as frisée and radicchio, which will stand up well to the heat of the salmon and contrast well with the sweetness of the sauce.

Using a sharp knife, cut the bone away from each salmon steak to create 8 salmon fillets. Shape the salmon fillets into noisettes and secure with fine string.

Mix together the citrus zests and juices, olive oil, honey, wholegrain mustard, salt and pepper in a shallow dish. Add the salmon fillets and turn to coat. Cover and leave to marinate in the refrigerator for 4 hours, turning them occasionally in the marinade.

Heat the wok, then add the groundnut oil and heat until hot. Lift out the salmon noisettes, reserving the marinade. Add the salmon to the wok and cook for 6–10 minutes, turning once during cooking, until cooked and the fish is just flaking. Pour the marinade into the wok and heat through gently.

Mix together the salad leaves, watercress and tomatoes and arrange on serving plates. Top with the salmon noisettes and drizzle over any remaining warm marinade. Serve immediately.

Zesty Whole-baked Salmon

INGREDIENTS   **SERVES 8**

Preheat the oven to 220°C/425°F/Gas Mark 7. Lightly rinse the fish and pat dry with absorbent kitchen paper. Season the cavity with a little salt and pepper. Make several diagonal cuts across the flesh of the fish and season.

Mix together the low-fat spread, garlic, lemon and orange zest and juice, nutmeg, mustard and fresh breadcrumbs. Mix well together. Spoon the breadcrumb mixture into the slits with a small sprig of dill. Place the remaining herbs inside the fish cavity. Weigh the fish and calculate the cooking time. Allow 10 minutes per 450 g/1 lb.

Lay the fish on a double thickness of kitchen foil. If liked, smear the fish with a little low-fat spread. Top with the lime slices and fold the foil into a parcel. Chill in the refrigerator for about 15 minutes.

Place in a roasting tin and cook in the preheated oven for the calculated cooking time. Fifteen minutes before the end of cooking, open the foil and return to the oven until the skin begins to crisp. Remove the fish from the oven and stand for 10 minutes.

Pour the juices from the roasting tin into a saucepan. Bring to the boil and stir in the crème fraîche and fromage frais. Simmer for 3 minutes, or until hot. Garnish with dill sprigs and serve immediately.

1.8 kg/4 lb whole salmon, cleaned

sea salt and freshly ground black pepper

50 g/2 oz low-fat spread

1 garlic clove, peeled and finely sliced

zest and juice of 1 lemon

zest of 1 orange

1 tsp freshly grated nutmeg

3 tbsp Dijon mustard

2 tbsp fresh white breadcrumbs

2 bunches fresh dill

1 bunch fresh tarragon

1 lime, sliced

150 ml/¼ pint half-fat crème fraîche

450 ml/¾ pint fromage frais

dill sprigs, to garnish

FOOD FACT

Scottish wild salmon is one of the finest in the world and much sought-after. However, it is harder to come by today so farmed salmon will be the more available option. Though farmed salmon is less good, properly sourced it can still be of very high quality, the Shetland Islands producing some of the best.

Fish Roulades with Rice & Spinach

INGREDIENTS   SERVES 4

4 × 175 g/6 oz lemon sole, skinned

salt and freshly ground black pepper

1 tsp fennel seeds

75 g/3 oz long-grain rice, cooked

150 g/5 oz white crab meat, fresh or canned

125 g/4 oz baby spinach, washed
and trimmed

5 tbsp dry white wine

5 tbsp half-fat crème fraîche

2 tbsp freshly chopped parsley,
plus extra to garnish

asparagus spears, to serve

Wipe each fish fillet with either a clean damp cloth or kitchen paper. Place on a chopping board, skinned side up, and season lightly with salt and black pepper.

Place the fennel seeds in a pestle and mortar and crush lightly. Transfer to a small bowl and stir in the cooked rice. Drain the crab meat thoroughly. Add to the rice mixture and mix lightly.

Lay 2–3 spinach leaves over each fillet and top with a quarter of the crab meat mixture. Roll up and secure with a cocktail stick if necessary. Place into a large pan and pour over the wine. Cover and cook on a medium heat for 5–7 minutes until cooked.

Remove the fish from the cooking liquor and transfer to a serving plate and keep warm. Stir the crème fraîche into the cooking liquor and season to taste. Heat for 3 minutes, then stir in the chopped parsley.

Spoon the sauce onto the base of a plate. Cut each roulade into slices and arrange on top of the sauce. Serve with freshly cooked asparagus spears.

Traditional Fish Pie

INGREDIENTS   **SERVES 4**

Preheat the oven to 200°C/400°F/Gas Mark 6, about 15 minutes before cooking. Place the fish in a shallow frying pan, pour over 300 ml/½ pint of the milk and add the onion. Season to taste with salt and pepper. Bring to the boil and simmer for 8–10 minutes until the fish is cooked. Remove the fish with a slotted spoon and place in a 1.5 litre/2½ pint baking dish. Strain the cooking liquid and reserve.

Boil the potatoes until soft, then mash with 40 g/1½ oz of the butter and 2–3 tablespoons of the remaining milk. Reserve.

Arrange the prawns and sliced eggs on top of the fish, then scatter over the sweetcorn and sprinkle with the parsley.

Melt the remaining butter in a saucepan, stir in the flour and cook gently for 1 minute, stirring. Whisk in the reserved cooking liquid and remaining milk. Cook for 2 minutes, or until thickened, then pour over the fish mixture and cool slightly.

Spread the mashed potato over the top of the pie and sprinkle over the grated cheese. Bake in the preheated oven for 30 minutes until golden. Serve immediately.

INGREDIENTS
450 g/1 lb cod or coley fillets, skinned
450 ml/¾ pint milk
1 small onion, peeled and quartered
salt and freshly ground black pepper
900 g/2 lb potatoes, peeled and cut into chunks
100 g/3½ oz butter
125 g/4 oz large prawns
2 large eggs, hard-boiled and quartered
198 g can sweetcorn, drained
2 tbsp freshly chopped parsley
3 tbsp plain flour
50 g/2 oz Cheddar cheese, grated

TASTY TIP

Any variety of white fish may be used in this delicious dish, including haddock, hake, ling, pollack and whiting. You could also used smoked fish, such as smoked cod or haddock, for a change. After simmering in milk, carefully check and remove any bones from the cooked fish.

Smoked Mackerel & Potato Salad

INGREDIENTS   SERVES 4

½ tsp dry mustard powder

1 large egg yolk

salt and freshly ground black pepper

150 ml/¼ pint sunflower oil

1–2 tbsp lemon juice

450 g/1 lb baby new potatoes

25 g/1 oz butter

350 g/12 oz smoked mackerel fillets

4 celery stalks, trimmed and finely chopped

3 tbsp creamed horseradish

150 ml/¼ pint crème fraîche

1 little gem lettuce, rinsed and roughly torn

8 cherry tomatoes, halved

HELPFUL HINT

When making mayonnaise, ensure that the ingredients are at room temperature, or it may curdle. For speed, it can be made in a food processor: briefly blend the mustard, yolk, seasoning and lemon juice, then, with the motor running, slowly pour in the oil.

Place the mustard powder and egg yolk in a small bowl with salt and pepper and whisk until blended. Add the oil, drop by drop, into the egg mixture, whisking continuously. When the mayonnaise is thick, add the lemon juice, drop by drop, until a smooth, glossy consistency is formed. Reserve.

Cook the potatoes in boiling salted water until tender, then drain. Cool slightly, then cut into halves or quarters, depending on size. Return to the saucepan and toss in the butter.

Remove the skin from the mackerel fillets and flake into pieces. Add to the potatoes in the saucepan, together with the celery.

Blend 4 tablespoons of the mayonnaise with the horseradish and crème fraîche. Season to taste with salt and pepper, then add to the potato and mackerel mixture and stir lightly.

Arrange the lettuce and tomatoes on 4 serving plates. Pile the smoked mackerel mixture on top of the lettuce, grind over a little pepper and serve with the remaining mayonnaise.

Luxury Fish Pasties

INGREDIENTS　　　　　**SERVES 6**

Preheat the oven to 200°C/400°F/Gas Mark 6. Place the butter in a saucepan and slowly heat until melted. Add the flour and cook, stirring, for 1 minute. Remove from the heat and gradually add the milk a little at a time, stirring between each addition.

Return to the heat and simmer, stirring continuously, until thickened. Remove from the heat and add the salmon, parsley, dill, lime zest, lime juice, prawns and seasoning.

Roll out the pastry on a lightly floured surface and cut out 6 x 12.5 cm/5 inch circles and 6 x 15 cm/6 inch circles. Brush the edges of the smallest circles with some beaten egg and place two tablespoons of filling in the centre of each one. Place the larger circles over the filling and press the edges together to seal. Pinch the edge of the pastry between the forefinger and thumb to ensure a firm seal and decorative edge.

Cut a slit in each parcel, brush with beaten egg and sprinkle with sea salt. Transfer to a baking sheet and cook in the preheated oven for 20 minutes, or until golden brown. Serve immediately with some fresh green salad leaves.

550 g/1¼ lb ready-made quick flaky pastry
125 g/4 oz butter
125 g/4 oz plain flour
300 ml/½ pint milk
225 g/8 oz salmon fillet, skinned and cut into chunks
1 tbsp freshly chopped parsley
1 tbsp freshly chopped dill
grated zest and juice of 1 lime
225 g/8 oz peeled and de-veined prawns
salt and freshly ground black pepper
1 small egg, beaten
1 tsp sea salt
fresh green salad leaves, to serve

Seared Scallop Salad

INGREDIENTS   **SERVES 4**

12 king (large) scallops

1 tbsp low-fat spread or butter

2 tbsp orange juice

2 tbsp balsamic vinegar

1 tbsp clear honey

2 ripe pears, washed

125 g/4 oz rocket

125 g/4 oz watercress

50 g/2 oz walnuts

freshly ground black pepper

Clean the scallops, removing the thin black vein from around the white meat and coral. Rinse thoroughly and dry on absorbent kitchen paper. Cut into 2–3 thick slices, depending on the scallop size.

Heat a griddle pan or heavy-based frying pan, then, when hot, add the low-fat spread or butter and allow to melt. Once melted, sear the scallops for 1 minute on each side, or until golden. Remove from the pan and reserve.

Briskly whisk together the orange juice, balsamic vinegar and honey to make the dressing and reserve.

With a small sharp knife, carefully cut the pears into quarters, core, then cut into chunks. Mix the rocket leaves, watercress, pear chunks and walnuts. Pile onto serving plates and top with the scallops. Drizzle over the dressing and grind over plenty of black pepper. Serve immediately.

Scallop & Potato Gratin

INGREDIENTS   SERVES 4

Preheat the oven to 220°C/425°F/Gas Mark 7. Clean 4 scallop shells to use as serving dishes and reserve. Place the scallops in a small saucepan with the wine, 150 ml/¼ pint water and salt and pepper. Cover and simmer very gently for 5 minutes, or until just tender. Remove with a slotted spoon and cut each scallop into 3 pieces. Reserve the cooking juices.

Melt 25 g/1 oz of the butter in a saucepan, stir in the flour and cook for 1 minute, stirring, then gradually whisk in the reserved cooking juices. Simmer, stirring, for 3–4 minutes until the sauce has thickened. Season to taste with salt and pepper. Remove from the heat and stir in the cream and 25 g/1 oz of the grated cheese. Fold in the scallops.

Boil the potatoes in lightly salted water until tender, then mash with the remaining butter and the milk. Spoon or pipe the mashed potato around the edges of the cleaned scallop shells.

Divide the scallop mixture between the 4 shells, placing the mixture neatly in the centre. Sprinkle with the remaining grated cheese and bake in the preheated oven for about 10–15 minutes until golden brown and bubbling. Serve immediately.

---

8 fresh scallops in their shells, cleaned

4 tbsp white wine

salt and freshly ground black pepper

50 g/2 oz butter

3 tbsp plain flour

2 tbsp single cream

50 g/2 oz Cheddar cheese, grated

450 g/1 lb potatoes, peeled and cut into chunks

1 tbsp milk

HELPFUL HINT

You can ask your fishmonger to open and clean the scallops if you plan to cook them on the same day. Alternatively, buy scallops live and keep in the refrigerator for up to 24 hours. The simplest and safest way to open scallops is to place them flat-side up on a baking sheet and put in a hot oven for a few minutes. Prise open the 2 shells and remove the white scallop meat and the bright orange coral.

VEGETABLES

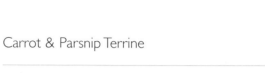

Carrot & Parsnip Terrine

INGREDIENTS   SERVES 8–10

550 g/1¼ lb carrots, peeled and chopped

450 g/1 lb parsnips, peeled and chopped

6 tbsp half-fat crème fraîche

450 g/1 lb spinach, rinsed

1 tbsp brown sugar

1 tbsp freshly chopped parsley

½ tsp freshly grated nutmeg

salt and freshly ground black pepper

6 medium eggs

fresh basil sprigs, to garnish

For the tomato coulis:

450 g/1 lb ripe tomatoes, deseeded and chopped

1 medium onion, peeled and finely chopped

Preheat the oven to 200°C/400°F/Gas Mark 6. Oil and line a 900 g/2 lb loaf tin with nonstick baking paper. Cook the carrots and parsnips in boiling salted water for 10–15 minutes until very tender. Drain and purée separately. Add 2 tablespoons of crème fraîche to both the carrots and the parsnips.

Steam the spinach for 5–10 minutes until very tender. Drain and squeeze out as much liquid as possible, then stir in the remaining crème fraîche.

Add the brown sugar to the carrot purée, the parsley to the parsnip mixture and the nutmeg to the spinach. Season all to taste with salt and pepper.

Beat 2 eggs, add to the spinach and turn into the prepared tin. Add another 2 beaten eggs to the carrot mixture and layer carefully on top of the spinach. Beat the remaining eggs into the parsnip purée and layer on top of the terrine.

Place the tin in a baking dish and pour in enough hot water to come halfway up the sides of the tin. Bake in the preheated oven for 1 hour until a skewer inserted into the centre comes out clean. Leave the terrine to cool for at least 30 minutes. Run a sharp knife around the edges. Turn out onto a dish and reserve.

Make the tomato coulis by simmering the tomatoes and onion together for 5–10 minutes until slightly thickened. Season to taste. Blend well in a liquidiser or food processor and serve as an accompaniment to the terrine. Garnish with basil sprigs and serve.

Clapshot

INGREDIENTS　　　　**SERVES 4**

450 g/1 lb potatoes, peeled

450 g/1 lb swede or turnips, peeled

2 tbsp chopped chives

65 g/2½ oz butter

salt and freshly ground black pepper, to taste

Boil the potatoes and swede or turnips in a large pan of lightly salted water for 15–20 minutes until tender. Drain, then mash the two vegetables together while still hot and mix in the butter, chives and seasoning.

Continue beating until smooth, or until you have the desired consistency. If necessary, continue to beat in a saucepan to ensure that it is piping hot before serving.

FOOD FACT

This is a tasty all-in-one version of the mashed 'neeps and tatties' that traditionally accompany haggis.

Kailkenny

Cut the potatoes into halves or quarters, depending on size. Put them into a large pan of salted water. Boil until cooked through and soft (about 35 minutes).

Meanwhile, cook the cabbage or kale. Either boil in water or steam in a steamer or colander above boiling water until tender. Drain well and chop finely.

Drain the potatoes, then mash them thoroughly and mix in the cooked cabbage or kale (saving some for garnish, if liked). Stir in the double cream, season with salt and pepper and serve immediately.

INGREDIENTS　　　　　**SERVES 2**

225 g/8 oz potatoes, peeled

225 g/8 oz cabbage or kale, leaves separated and rinsed

125 ml/4 fl oz double cream

salt and freshly ground black pepper, to taste

FOOD FACT

Kailkenny is an Aberdeenshire version of the Scottish dish 'rumbledethumps', which itself is very similar to the Irish dish 'colcannon'. Kailkenny uses cream, instead of the usual butter.

Leek & Potato Tart

Preheat the oven to 200°C/400°F/Gas Mark 6, about 15 minutes before baking. Sift the flour and salt into a bowl. Rub in the butter until the mixture resembles breadcrumbs. Stir in the nuts. Mix together the egg yolk and 3 tablespoons cold water. Sprinkle over the dry ingredients. Mix to form a dough.

Knead on a lightly floured surface for a few seconds, then wrap in clingfilm and chill in the refrigerator for 20 minutes. Roll out and use to line a 20.5 cm/8 inch spring-form tin or very deep flan tin. Chill for a further 30 minutes.

Cook the leeks in the butter over a high heat for 2–3 minutes, stirring constantly. Lower the heat, cover and cook for 25 minutes until soft, stirring occasionally. Remove the leeks from the heat.

Cook the potatoes in boiling salted water for 15 minutes, or until almost tender. Drain and thickly slice. Add to the leeks. Stir the soured cream into the leeks and potatoes, followed by the eggs, cheese, nutmeg and salt and pepper. Pour into the pastry case and bake on the middle shelf in the preheated oven for 20 minutes.

Reduce the oven temperature to 190°C/375°F/Gas Mark 5 and cook for a further 30–35 minutes, or until the filling is set. Garnish with chives and serve immediately.

225 g/8 oz plain flour

pinch salt

150 g/5 oz butter, cubed

50 g/2 oz walnuts, very finely chopped

I large egg yolk

For the filling:

450 g/I lb leeks, trimmed and thinly sliced

40 g/I½ oz butter

450 g/I lb large new potatoes, scrubbed

300 ml/½ pint soured cream

3 medium eggs, lightly beaten

175 g/6 oz Gruyère cheese, grated

freshly grated nutmeg

salt and freshly ground black pepper

fresh chives, to garnish

TASTY TIP

To ring the changes, flavour the pastry with different nuts, such as hazelnuts or almonds, or replace the nuts with 3 tablespoons of freshly chopped mixed herbs.

Cheese & Onion Oat Pie

INGREDIENTS SERVES 4

I tbsp sunflower oil, plus I tsp

25 g/I oz butter

2 medium onions, peeled and sliced

I garlic clove, peeled and crushed

150 g/5 oz porridge oats

125 g/4 oz mature Cheddar cheese, grated

2 medium eggs, lightly beaten

2 tbsp freshly chopped parsley

salt and freshly ground black pepper

275 g/10 oz baking potato, peeled

Preheat the oven to 180°C/350°F/Gas Mark 4. Heat the oil and half the butter in a saucepan until melted. Add the onions and garlic and cook gently for 10 minutes, or until soft. Remove from the heat and tip into a large bowl.

Spread the oats out on a baking sheet and toast in the hot oven for 12 minutes. Leave to cool, then add to the onions with the cheese, eggs and parsley. Season to taste with salt and pepper and mix well.

Line the base of a 20.5 cm/8 inch round sandwich tin with greaseproof paper and oil well. Thinly slice the potato and arrange the slices on the base, overlapping them slightly.

Spoon the cheese and oat mixture on top of the potato, spreading evenly with the back of a spoon. Cover with kitchen foil and bake for 30 minutes.

Invert the pie onto a baking sheet so that the potato slices are on top. Carefully remove the tin and lining paper.

Preheat the grill to medium. Melt the remaining butter and carefully brush over the potato topping. Cook under the preheated grill for 5–6 minutes until the potatoes are lightly browned. Cut into wedges and serve.

DESSERTS

Cranachan

75 g/3 oz pinhead or coarse oatmeal

300 ml/½ pint double cream

2 tbsp honey

1 tbsp Drambuie, or few drops
vanilla essence

175 g/6 oz fresh raspberries

Toast the oatmeal in a frying pan, stirring continuously, on a medium heat for 10–20 minutes until lightly browned. Transfer to a plate and allow to cool.

Whisk the cream into a soft consistency and mix in most of the oatmeal (reserving some for decoration), honey and Drambuie (alternatively, use a few drops vanilla essence or other flavouring of your choice).

Put a few of the raspberries in the bottoms of two tall serving glasses and save a few for decoration. Fold the rest of the raspberries into the cream mixture, crushing some of them slightly to add a pink tinge to the cream. (Alternatively, crush the raspberries, add a layer to the glasses, top with cream, add another layer of raspberries and finish with a layer of cream.)

Smooth the tops, decorate with the reserved oatmeal and raspberries and serve.

TASTY TIP
Cranachan can be frozen for a more ice-cream-like dessert.

Crème Brûlée with Sugared Raspberries

INGREDIENTS **SERVES 6**

600 ml/1 pint fresh whipping cream

4 medium egg yolks

75 g/3 oz caster sugar

½ tsp vanilla essence

25 g/1 oz demerara sugar

175 g/6 oz fresh raspberries

Preheat the oven to 150°C/300°F/Gas Mark 2. Pour the cream into a bowl and place over a saucepan of gently simmering water. Heat gently but do not allow to boil.

Meanwhile, whisk together the egg yolks, 50 g/2 oz of the caster sugar and the vanilla essence. When the cream is warm, pour it over the egg mixture, briskly whisking until it is mixed completely. Pour into 6 individual ramekin dishes and place in a roasting tin. Fill the tin with sufficient water to come halfway up the sides of the dishes. Bake in the preheated oven for about 1 hour, or until the puddings are set. (To test if set, carefully insert a round-bladed knife into the centre; if the knife comes out clean, they are set.)

Remove the puddings from the roasting tin and allow to cool. Chill in the refrigerator, preferably overnight. Sprinkle the sugar over the top of each dish and place the puddings under a preheated hot grill. When the sugar has caramelised and turned deep brown, remove from the heat and cool. Chill the puddings in the refrigerator for 2–3 hours before serving. Toss the raspberries in the remaining caster sugar and sprinkle over the top of each dish. Serve with a little extra cream, if liked.

FOOD FACT

Although this dish probably originates in France and has been argued to have roots in Cambridge, England, it can also be traced back to eighteenth-century Aberdeenshire and has long been enjoyed in Scotland.

Cloutie Dumpling

INGREDIENTS   SERVES 6

225 g/8 oz plain flour

125 g/4 oz shredded suet or margarine
(margarine makes a lighter dumpling)

125 g/4 oz oatmeal

75 g/3 oz sugar

1 rounded tsp baking powder

225 g/8 oz mixed currants, sultanas
and raisins

1–1½ tsp each ground cinnamon
and mixed spice

2 eggs, beaten

1 tsp golden syrup

3–4 tbsp buttermilk

FOOD FACT

Much like the more well-known
English dessert, 'Christmas Pudding',
Cloutie Dumpling is traditionally made
at Christmas time, when trinkets, coins
and lucky gifts are sometimes dropped
into the mixture, wrapped in
greaseproof paper. It is also made for
other special occasions such as a
birthday or Hogmanay, as well as
being enjoyed throughout the year.

Sift the flour and rub in the suet or margarine in a large mixing bowl. Add all the other dry ingredients, including the fruit, and mix with a wooden spoon.

Make a well in the centre and add the eggs and syrup and mix well. Add enough buttermilk to make a soft but firm batter.

Lightly grease a pudding basin with melted butter and pour the pudding in. Allow a 2 cm/1 inch space at the top, even if this means throwing away some of the mixture – you will need the space for expansion.

Cover the basin with a greased sheet of foil or greaseproof paper and secure with string, place the basin in a large saucepan and pour boiling water into a saucepan until it comes two thirds of the way up the side. Boil for 3 hours.

Alternatively, cook the dumpling the traditional way – i.e. in a muslin cloth (or 'clout', hence the name). A tea towel can also be used. Dip in boiling water and flour well before adding the mixture. Tie the top, leaving room for expansion, then place on a plate in a saucepan. Cover with boiling water and cook for 2½–3 hours.

Turn out the dumpling and serve either hot with custard or cold with cream. (If it has been cooked in a cloth, you could dry its 'skin' in the oven first.)

Crunchy Rhubarb Crumble

INGREDIENTS   **SERVES 4**

Preheat the oven to 180°C/350°F/Gas Mark 4. Place the flour in a large bowl and cut the butter into cubes. Add to the flour and rub in with the fingertips until the mixture looks like fine breadcrumbs, or blend for a few seconds in a food processor.

Stir in the rolled oats, demerara sugar, sesame seeds and cinnamon. Mix well and reserve.

Prepare the rhubarb by removing the thick ends of the stalks and cut diagonally into 2.5 cm/1 inch chunks. Wash thoroughly and pat dry with a clean tea towel. Place the rhubarb in a 1.1 litre/2 pint pie dish.

Sprinkle the caster sugar over the rhubarb and top with the reserved crumble mixture. Level the top of the crumble so that all the fruit is well covered and press down firmly. If liked, sprinkle the top with a little extra caster sugar.

Place on a baking sheet and bake in the preheated oven for 40–50 minutes, or until the fruit is soft and the topping is golden brown. Sprinkle the pudding with some more caster sugar and serve hot with custard or cream.

INGREDIENTS
125 g/4 oz plain flour
50 g/2 oz softened butter
50 g/2 oz rolled oats
50 g/2 oz demerara sugar
1 tbsp sesame seeds
½ tsp ground cinnamon
450 g/1 lb fresh rhubarb
50 g/2 oz caster sugar
custard or cream, to serve

Oaty Fruit Puddings

INGREDIENTS   **SERVES 4**

125 g/4 oz rolled oats

50 g/2 oz butter, melted

2 tbsp chopped almonds

1 tbsp clear honey

pinch ground cinnamon

2 pears, peeled, cored and finely chopped

1 tbsp marmalade

orange zest, to decorate

custard or fruit-flavoured yogurt, to serve

TASTY TIP

Liqueur custard is superb with steamed and baked puddings. Add 2–3 tablespoons of either Drambuie or a liqueur of your choice to the custard, together with 1 teaspoon of vanilla essence. Taste the custard and add more alcohol if desired.

Preheat the oven to 200°C/400°F/Gas Mark 6. Lightly oil and line the bases of 4 individual pudding bowls or muffin tins with a small circle of greaseproof paper.

Mix together the oats, butter, nuts, honey and cinnamon in a small bowl.

Using a spoon, spread two thirds of the oaty mixture over the base and around the sides of the pudding bowls or muffin tins.

Toss together the pears and marmalade and spoon into the oaty cases. Scatter over the remaining oaty mixture to cover the pears and marmalade. Bake in the preheated oven for 15–20 minutes until cooked and the tops of the puddings are golden and crisp.

Leave for 5 minutes before removing the pudding bowls or the muffin tins. Decorate with orange zest and serve hot with custard or fruit-flavoured yogurt.

Scotch Pancakes

INGREDIENTS   **SERVES 4**

Heat a griddle or heavy-based frying pan and lightly grease it.

Sift together the flour, salt, cream of tartar and bicarbonate of soda and mix in the caster sugar.

Create a well in the centre and add the egg and some of the milk. Slowly mix the flour into the egg and milk, adding more milk as you go until you have a mixture with the consistency of thick batter.

Drop a small amount of batter onto the greased griddle or pan – if it is the right temperature, bubbles should rise to the top in a few seconds. Drop in enough mixture to make several individual small pancakes.

When the underside is brown and bubbles are bursting on the top, turn the pancakes over and cook the other side. You may need to re-grease the pan after each batch.

Serve warm with butter, and honey or jam. They are also delicious buttered and sprinkled with light brown sugar.

225 g/8 oz plain flour
pinch salt
1 tsp cream of tartar
1 tsp bicarbonate of soda
5 tsp caster sugar
1 medium egg
150 ml/¼ pint milk

Dornoch Dreams

INGREDIENTS SERVES 12

50 g/2 oz butter or margarine

175 ml/6 fl oz water

125 g/4 oz plain flour

3 eggs

350 g/12 oz raspberries
(whole or lightly crushed)

125 g/4 oz clear honey

300 ml/½ pint double cream

2 tbsp Drambuie

icing sugar, for decoration

Preheat the oven to 200°C/400°F/Gas Mark 6. Place the butter or margarine and water in a saucepan and heat until the fat has melted. Remove from the heat and stir in the flour.

Beat until the mixture forms a ball and leaves the edges of the pan cleanly. Beat the eggs and slowly add them, a little at a time, beating well between each addition until the mixture is smooth, shiny and of a piping consistency.

Spoon the pastry mixture into a large piping bag with a plain nozzle and pipe 12 round cakes onto a lightly greased baking tray.

Bake in the centre of the preheated oven for 20–30 minutes until golden brown. Remove from the oven, pierce to allow the steam to escape and then leave to cool.

Mix together the raspberries and honey in a bowl. Whip the cream and stir in the Drambuie, then split the buns and fill with the raspberries and cream. Dust with icing sugar and serve immediately.

Rice Pudding

INGREDIENTS   **SERVES 4**

Preheat the oven to 150°C/300°F/Gas Mark 2. Lightly oil an ovenproof dish.

Put the rice, milk and the lemon peel in a pot and heat gently until simmering. Cook for 10 minutes, stirring constantly to prevent sticking.

When the rice is soft, pour it into a baking dish and mix in the butter or shredded suet. Allow to cool to a warm temperature.

Add the beaten eggs, sugar and raisins, if using, to the pudding. Mix well. Sprinkle over the nutmeg. Cover with kitchen foil and bake the pudding in the preheated oven for 30 minutes, removing the foil for the last 10 minutes of baking. Serve warm with jam.

125 g/4 oz pudding rice

900 ml/1½ pints whole milk

1 piece lemon peel

50 g/2 oz butter or shredded suet

3 eggs, beaten

50–125 g/2–4 oz sugar, to taste

1 handful raisins (optional)

pinch freshly grated nutmeg

jam, to serve

TASTY TIP
If you prefer a thicker pudding, bake for longer. Check the pudding after the first 30 minutes and stir well before returning to the oven. Check and stir regularly until it has reached the desired consistency.

Summer Pudding

INGREDIENTS   SERVES 4

450 g/1 lb redcurrants

125 g/4 oz caster sugar

350 g/12 oz strawberries, hulled and halved

125 g/4 oz raspberries

2 tbsp Grand Marnier or Cointreau

8–10 medium slices white bread, crusts removed

mint sprigs, to decorate

Greek-style yogurt or fromage frais, to serve

Place the redcurrants, sugar and 1 tablespoon water in a large saucepan. Heat gently until the sugar has just dissolved and the juices have just begun to run.

Remove the saucepan from the heat and stir in the strawberries, raspberries and the Grand Marnier or Cointreau.

Line the base and sides of a 1.1 litre/2 pint pudding basin with two thirds of the bread, making sure that the slices overlap each other slightly.

Spoon the fruit with their juices into the bread-lined pudding basin, then top with the remaining bread slices.

Place a small plate on top of the pudding, so that it fits inside the pudding basin. Ensure the plate fits tightly, then weigh down with a clean can or some weights and chill in the refrigerator overnight.

When ready to serve, remove the weights and plate. Carefully loosen round the sides of the basin with a round-bladed knife. Invert the pudding onto a serving plate, decorate with the mint sprigs and serve with the yogurt or fromage frais.

BREADS & BAKING

Mixed Grain Bread

INGREDIENTS

MAKES 1 LARGE LOAF

350 g/12 oz strong white flour

2 tsp salt

225 g/8 oz strong Granary flour

125 g/4 oz rye flour

25 g/1 oz butter, diced

2 tsp easy-blend dried yeast

25 g/1 oz rolled oats

2 tbsp sunflower seeds

1 tbsp malt extract

450 ml/¾ pint warm water (see Helpful Hint)

1 medium egg, beaten

HELPFUL HINT

The amount of water you need to add to the dry ingredients in this recipe will depend on the type and brand of flour you use. Add just enough water to make a soft elastic dough.

Preheat the oven to 220°C/425°F/Gas Mark 7, 15 minutes before baking. Sift the white flour and salt into a large bowl. Stir in the Granary and rye flours, then rub in the butter until the mixture resembles breadcrumbs. Stir in the yeast, oats and seeds and make a well in the centre.

Stir the malt extract into the warm water until dissolved. Add the malt water to the dry ingredients. Mix to a soft dough.

Turn the dough out onto a lightly floured surface and knead for 10 minutes until smooth and elastic. Put in an oiled bowl, cover with clingfilm and leave to rise in a warm place for 1½ hours, or until doubled in size.

Turn out and knead again for a minute or two to knock out the air. Shape into an oval loaf about 30.5 cm/12 inches long and place on a well-oiled baking sheet. Cover with oiled clingfilm and leave to rise for 40 minutes, or until doubled in size.

Brush the loaf with beaten egg and bake in the preheated oven for 35–45 minutes, or until the bread is well risen, browned and sounds hollow when the base is tapped. Leave to cool on a wire rack, then serve.

Traditional Oven Scones

INGREDIENTS   **MAKES 8**

Preheat the oven to 220°C/425°F/Gas Mark 7, 15 minutes before baking. Sift the flour, baking powder and salt into a large bowl. Rub in the butter until the mixture resembles fine breadcrumbs. Stir in the sugar and mix in enough milk to give a fairly soft dough.

Knead the dough on a lightly floured surface for a few seconds until smooth. Roll out until 2 cm/¾ inches thick and stamp out 6.5 cm/2½ inch rounds with a floured plain cutter.

Place on an oiled baking sheet and brush the tops with milk (do not brush it over the sides or the scones will not rise properly). Dust with a little plain flour.

Bake in the preheated oven for 12–15 minutes, or until well risen and golden brown. Transfer to a wire rack and serve warm or leave to cool completely. (The scones are best eaten on the day of baking but may be kept in an airtight tin for up to 2 days.)

For lemon-and-sultana scones, stir in the sultanas and lemon zest with the sugar. Roll out until 2 cm/¾ inches thick and cut into 8 fingers, 10 x 2.5 cm/ 4 x 1 inch in size. Brush with a little beaten egg and bake the scones as before.

225 g/8 oz self-raising flour

1 tsp baking powder

pinch salt

40 g/1½ oz butter, cubed

15 g/½ oz caster sugar

150 ml/¼ pint milk, plus 1 tbsp for brushing

1 tbsp plain flour, to dust

For a lemon-and-sultana scone variation:

50 g/2 oz sultanas

finely grated zest of ½ lemon

beaten egg, to glaze

TASTY TIP

A frequently repeated legend is that the scone takes its name from the Stone of Scone (pronounced 'Scoone'), or 'Stone of Destiny', which used to be kept at the now-ruined abbey in Scone, near Perth. Whatever the origins, scones have been made in Scotland for centuries, originally starting life as a large round 'bannock' that would be cut into quadrants.

Cheese-crusted Potato Scones

INGREDIENTS   MAKES 6

200 g/7 oz self-raising flour

25 g/1 oz wholemeal flour

½ tsp salt

1½ tsp baking powder

25 g/1 oz butter, cubed

5 tbsp milk

175 g/6 oz cold mashed potato

freshly ground black pepper

To finish:

2 tbsp milk

40 g/1½ oz mature Cheddar cheese, finely grated

paprika, to dust

basil sprig, to garnish

Preheat the oven to 220°C/425°F/Gas Mark 7, 15 minutes before baking. Sift the flours, salt and baking powder into a large bowl. Rub in the butter until the mixture resembles fine breadcrumbs.

Stir 4 tablespoons of the milk into the mashed potato and season with black pepper. Add the dry ingredients to the potato mixture, mixing together with a fork and adding the remaining 1 tablespoon of milk if needed.

Knead the dough on a lightly floured surface for a few seconds until smooth. Roll out to a 15 cm/6 inch round and transfer to an oiled baking sheet. Mark the scone round into 6 wedges, cutting about halfway through with a small sharp knife. Brush with milk, then sprinkle with the cheese and a faint dusting of paprika. Bake on the middle shelf of the preheated oven for 15 minutes, or until well risen and golden brown. Transfer to a wire rack and leave to cool for 5 minutes before breaking into wedges.

Serve warm or leave to cool completely. Once cool, store the scones in an airtight tin. Garnish with a basil sprig and serve split and buttered.

Oatcakes

INGREDIENTS
MAKES 4–8 CAKES

125 g/4 oz medium oatmeal, plus extra for kneading

pinch salt

pinch bicarbonate of soda

2 tsp melted fat (use bacon dripping, if possible)

3–4 tbsp hot water

HELPFUL HINT
Oatcakes are the 'national bread of Scotland'. Traditionally, each community had its own mill to grind oats from local crofts and supply oatmeal to every household. These oats formed the Highlanders' staple diet of porridge and oatcakes.

Preheat a heavy-based frying pan or griddle over a medium-high heat and lightly grease. Put the oatmeal, salt and bicarbonate of soda in a large bowl and mix together. Make a well in the centre and pour in the melted fat. Stir well, then add enough of the hot water to make a stiff paste.

Scatter some extra oatmeal over a clean work surface and turn the paste out onto it. With your hands covered in oatmeal to prevent sticking, roll the paste into a ball and knead well. Try to work as quickly as you can because the mixture will stiffen if left for too long. Roll out the mixture evenly until about ½ cm/¼ inch thick. Take a small plate or saucer, place the plate on top of the mixture and cut around the edges to make a round.

Sprinkle the round with oatmeal and put in the frying pan or on the griddle. Cook for about 3 minutes until the edges curl slightly, then turn over and cook on the other side. Get ready with the next oatcake while the first one is cooking. Once cooked, the oatcakes can either be served immediately or stored in a tin and reheated in a moderate (180°C/350°F/ Gas Mark 4) oven or by lightly toasting, as required.

Oatmeal Coconut Cookies

INGREDIENTS　　　　**MAKES 40**

Preheat the oven to 180°C/350°F/Gas Mark 4, 10 minutes before baking. Lightly oil a baking sheet. Cream together the butter or margarine and sugars until light and fluffy. Gradually stir in the egg and vanilla essence and beat until well blended.

Sift together the flour, baking powder and bicarbonate of soda in another bowl. Add to the butter and sugar mixture and beat together until smooth. Fold in the rolled oats and coconut with a metal spoon or rubber spatula.

Roll heaped teaspoonfuls of the mixture into balls and place on the baking sheet about 5 cm/2 inches apart and flatten each ball slightly with the heel of the hand. Transfer to the preheated oven and bake for 12–15 minutes until just golden. Remove from the oven and transfer the biscuits to a wire rack to cool completely and serve.

Ingredients
225 g/8 oz butter or margarine
125 g/4 oz soft light brown sugar
125 g/4 oz caster sugar
1 large egg, lightly beaten
1 tsp vanilla essence
225 g/8 oz plain flour
1 tsp baking powder
½ tsp bicarbonate of soda
125 g/4 oz rolled oats
75 g/3 oz desiccated coconut

Oatmeal Raisin Cookies

INGREDIENTS   **MAKES 24**

Preheat the oven to 200°C/400°F/Gas Mark 6, 15 minutes before baking. Lightly oil a baking sheet.

Mix together the flour, oats, ground ginger, baking powder, bicarbonate of soda, sugar and the raisins in a large bowl.

In another bowl, mix the egg, oil and milk together. Make a well in the centre of the dry ingredients and pour in the egg mixture. Mix together well with either a fork or a wooden spoon to make a soft but not sticky dough.

Place spoonfuls of the dough well apart on the oiled baking sheet and flatten the tops down slightly with the tines of a fork. Transfer the biscuits to the preheated oven and bake for 10–12 minutes until golden. Remove from the oven, leave to cool for 2–3 minutes, then transfer the biscuits to a wire rack to cool. Serve when cold or store in an airtight tin.

INGREDIENTS
175 g/6 oz plain flour
150 g/5 oz rolled oats
1 tsp ground ginger
½ tsp baking powder
½ tsp bicarbonate of soda
125 g/4 oz soft light brown sugar
50 g/2 oz raisins
1 medium egg, lightly beaten
150 ml/¼ pint vegetable or sunflower oil
4 tbsp milk

HELPFUL HINT

This dough can be made, wrapped in clingfilm, then stored in the refrigerator for up to 1 week before baking. When ready to bake, simply cut off the dough and bake as above.

Fruit & Nut Flapjacks

INGREDIENTS   MAKES 12

75 g/3 oz butter or margarine

125 g/4 oz soft light brown sugar

3 tbsp golden syrup

50 g/2 oz raisins

50 g/2 oz walnuts, roughly chopped

175 g/6 oz rolled oats

50 g/2 oz icing sugar

1–1½ tbsp lemon juice

FOOD FACT
This is another way to make use of that iconic Scottish ingredient: oats. The rolled oats used in flapjacks can also be used when making porridge, as can oatmeal, which is an integral part of haggis, oatcakes and the whisky drink Atholl Brose: all great Scottish products.

Preheat the oven to 180°C/350°F/Gas Mark 4, 10 minutes before baking. Lightly oil a 23 cm/9 inch square cake tin.

Melt the butter or margarine with the sugar and syrup in a small saucepan over a low heat.

Remove from the heat. Stir the raisins, walnuts and oats into the syrup mixture and mix together well. Spoon evenly into the prepared tin and press down well. Transfer to the preheated oven and bake for 20–25 minutes.

Remove from the oven and leave to cool in the tin. Cut into bars while still warm.

Sift the icing sugar into a small bowl, then gradually beat in the lemon juice a little at a time to form a thin icing. Place into an icing bag fitted with a writing nozzle, then pipe thin lines over the flapjacks. Allow to cool and serve.

Shortbread Biscuits

INGREDIENTS   **MAKES 36**

Preheat the oven to 180°C/350°F/Gas Mark 4, 10 minutes before baking. Lightly oil a baking sheet.

Cream the butter and icing sugar until fluffy. Gradually add the flour and continue beating for a further 2–3 minutes until it is smooth and light. Roll into balls and place on a baking sheet.

Cover half of the dough mixture with hundreds and thousands, sugar strands, chocolate drops or silver balls. Keep the other half plain. Bake in the preheated oven for 6–8 minutes until the bottoms are lightly browned. Remove from the oven and transfer to a wire rack to cool.

Sift the icing sugar into a small bowl. Add the lemon juice and blend until a smooth icing forms. Using a small spoon, swirl the icing over the cooled plain biscuits. Decorate with the extra hundreds and thousands, chocolate drops or silver balls and serve.

225 g/8 oz butter, softened

75 g/3 oz icing sugar

175 g/6 oz flour

hundreds and thousands

sugar strands

chocolate drops

silver balls

50 g/2 oz icing sugar

2–3 tsp lemon juice

HELPFUL HINT

This is a variation on classic Scottish shortbread – they retain the flavour but the texture is much lighter. They literally melt in the mouth. These biscuits are great for children. However, for a smarter-looking biscuit which is more appealing to adults, spoon the mixture into a piping bag fitted with a large star nozzle and pipe the biscuits onto the baking sheet. Bake as above.

Pecan Caramel Millionaire's Shortbread

INGREDIENTS   MAKES 20

125 g/4 oz butter, softened

2 tbsp smooth peanut butter

75 g/3 oz caster sugar

75 g/3 oz cornflour

175 g/6 oz plain flour

For the topping:

200 g/7 oz caster sugar

125 g/4 oz butter

2 tbsp golden syrup

75 g/3 oz liquid glucose

75 ml/3 fl oz water

400 g can sweetened condensed milk

175 g/6 oz pecans, roughly chopped

75 g/3 oz plain dark chocolate

1 tbsp butter

TASTY TIP

Any type of nut can be used in this recipe. Why not try replacing the pecans with a variety of chopped walnuts, almonds and Brazil nuts?

Preheat the oven to 180°C/350°F/Gas Mark 4 10, minutes before baking. Lightly oil and line an 18 cm x 28 cm/7 x 11 inch tin with greaseproof or baking paper.

Cream together the butter, peanut butter and sugar until light. Sift in the cornflour and flour together and mix in to make a smooth dough. Press the mixture into the prepared tin and prick all over with a fork. Bake in the preheated oven for 20 minutes until just golden. Remove from the oven.

Meanwhile, for the topping, combine the sugar, butter, golden syrup, glucose, water and milk in a heavy-based saucepan. Stir constantly over a low heat without boiling until the sugar has dissolved. Increase the heat, boil steadily, stirring constantly, for about 10 minutes until the mixture turns a golden caramel colour. Remove the saucepan from the heat and add the pecans. Pour over the shortbread base immediately. Allow to cool, then refrigerate for at least 1 hour.

Break the chocolate into small pieces and put into a heatproof bowl with the butter. Place over a saucepan of barely simmering water, ensuring that the bowl does not come into contact with the water. Leave until melted, then stir together well.

Remove the shortbread from the refrigerator and pour the chocolate evenly over the top, spreading thinly to cover. Leave to set, cut into squares and serve.

Shortbread Thumbs

INGREDIENTS   MAKES 12

Preheat the oven to 150°C/300°F/Gas Mark 2, 10 minutes before baking. Lightly oil 2 baking sheets. Sift the flour into a large bowl, cut 75 g/3 oz of the butter and the white vegetable fat into small cubes, add to the flour, then, using your fingertips, rub in until the mixture resembles fine breadcrumbs.

Stir in the granulated sugar, sifted cornflour and 4 tablespoons of cocoa powder and bring the mixture together with your hand to form a soft and pliable dough.

Place on a lightly floured surface and shape into 12 small balls. Place onto the baking sheets at least 5 cm/2 inches apart, then press each one with a clean thumb to make a dent.

Bake in the preheated oven for 20–25 minutes until light golden brown. Remove from the oven and leave for 1–2 minutes to cool and not for longer, as they will continue to cook and could overcook. Transfer to a wire rack and leave until cold.

Sift the icing sugar and the remaining cocoa powder into a bowl and add the remaining softened butter. Blend to form a smooth and spreadable icing with 1–2 tablespoons hot water. Spread a little icing over the top of each biscuit and place half a cherry on each. Leave until set before serving.

INGREDIENTS
125 g/4 oz self-raising flour
125 g/4 oz butter, softened
25 g/1 oz white vegetable fat
50 g/2 oz granulated sugar
25 g/1 oz cornflour, sifted
5 tbsp cocoa powder, sifted
125 g/4 oz icing sugar
6 assorted coloured glacé cherries, rinsed, dried and halved

FOOD FACT
Using a combination of butter and vegetable fat gives these biscuits a softer texture than using all butter.

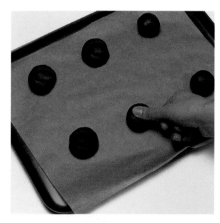

Dundee Cake

INGREDIENTS
CUTS INTO 10 SLICES

175 g/6 oz butter or margarine

150 g/5 oz caster or granulated sugar

4 eggs

225 g/8 oz plain flour

40 g/1½ oz mixed peel

175 g/6 oz each currants, raisins and sultanas

grated zest and juice of 1 lemon

1 level tsp baking powder

2 tbsp whisky

25 g/1 oz blanched almonds

2 tbsp boiled milk

1 tbsp sugar

Preheat the oven to 170°C/325°F/Gas Mark 3. Cream the butter and sugar in a bowl. When they are light and fluffy, slowly add the 4 eggs, one at a time, plus a spoonful of flour with each, beating well all the time.

Stir in the mixed peel and dried fruit and the lemon zest and juice. Add the rest of the flour, sifted with the baking powder, and the whisky. Make sure the mixture is stirred well. If it is too stiff, add a little milk.

Place the mixture in a 20 cm/8 inch greased and lined cake tin and flatten the top with a spoon. Cover with foil or greaseproof paper and bake in the preheated oven for 2 hours. Halfway through the cooking time, take off the foil and arrange the split almonds in concentric circles on the top of the cake. Check the cake with a skewer towards the end of cooking. If it is still uncooked in the middle, put it back for the rest of the 2 hours. About 5–10 minutes before the end of the cooking time, mix the boiled milk with the sugar. Brush the top with the sweetened milk to create a dry glaze. Keep in the tin for 15 minutes before turning out on a wire rack and store in an airtight container when cool.

Black Bun

INGREDIENTS   **SERVES 6–8**

Preheat the oven to 160°C/325°F/Gas Mark 3. Grease a 20 cm/8 inch loaf tin. Rub the fats into the flour and salt and then mix in enough cold water to make a stiff dough – this will be lining the tin.

Roll out the pastry and cut into six pieces, using the bottom, top and four sides of the tin as a rough guide. Press the bottom and four side pieces into the tin, pressing the overlaps to seal the pastry shell.

Mix the raisins, currants, almonds, mixed peel and sugar together. Sift in the flour, all the spices and the baking powder and bind them together using the brandy and almost all the egg. Add enough milk to keep the mixture moist.

Pack the filling into the lined tin and add the pastry lid, pinching the edges and using milk or egg to seal really well. Lightly prick the surface with a fork and make four holes to the bottom of the tin with a skewer. Make a small depression in the centre, as it will rise as it cooks. Brush the top with milk or the rest of the egg to create a glaze. Bake in the preheated oven for 2 1/2–3 hours. Test with a skewer – if it does not come out clean, continue cooking. Cool in the tin and then turn onto a wire rack.

For the pastry case:

75 g/3 oz lard

75 g/3 oz butter

350 g/12 oz plain flour

pinch salt

For the filling:

450 g/1 lb raisins

450 g/1 lb currants

50 g/2 oz blanched almonds, chopped

50 g/2 oz mixed peel, chopped

75 g/3 oz soft brown sugar

175 g/6 oz plain flour

1 level tsp ground allspice

½ level tsp each ground ginger, ground cinnamon, baking powder

1 generous pinch black pepper

½ tsp baking powder

1 tbsp brandy

1 large egg, beaten

milk, to moisten

Coconut & Almond Munchies

INGREDIENTS MAKES 26–30

Preheat the oven to 150°C/300°F/Gas Mark 2, 10 minutes before baking. Line several baking sheets with rice paper. Place the egg whites in a clean, grease-free bowl and whisk until stiff and standing in peaks. Sift the icing sugar, then carefully fold half of the sugar into the whisked egg whites together with the ground almonds. Add the coconut, the remaining icing sugar and the lemon zest and mix together to form a very sticky dough.

Place the mixture in a piping bag and pipe the mixture into walnut-sized mounds onto the rice paper, then sprinkle with a little extra icing sugar. Bake in the preheated oven for 20–25 minutes, or until set and golden on the outside. Remove from the oven and leave to cool slightly. Using a spatula, carefully transfer to a wire rack and leave until cold.

Break the milk and white chocolate into pieces and place in 2 separate bowls. Melt both chocolates set over saucepans of gently simmering water. Alternatively, melt in the microwave, according to the manufacturer's instructions. Stir until smooth and free from lumps. Dip one edge of each munchie in the milk chocolate and leave to dry on nonstick baking parchment. When dry, dip the other side into the white chocolate. Leave to set, then serve as soon as possible.

INGREDIENTS
5 medium egg whites
250 g/9 oz icing sugar, plus extra to sprinkle
225 g/8 oz ground almonds
200 g/7 oz desiccated coconut
grated zest of 1 lemon
125 g/4 oz milk chocolate
125 g/4 oz white chocolate

HELPFUL HINT

A 'macaroon' in Scotland can mean a sweet confection with a fondant centre. The munchies shown here are more like the more well-known coconut macaroon, also said to have been invented in Govan, Glasgow, Scotland.

Honey Cake

50 g/2 oz butter

25 g/1 oz caster sugar

125 g/4 oz clear heather honey

175 g/6 oz plain flour

½ tsp bicarbonate of soda

½ tsp mixed spice

1 medium egg

2 tbsp milk

25 g/1 oz flaked almonds

1 tbsp clear honey, to drizzle

TASTY TIP

Scottish heather honey captures the essence of the land with its rich, mellow flavour derived from the combination of ling and bell heathers found in profusion in the Highlands.

Preheat the oven to 180°C/350°F/Gas Mark 4, 10 minutes before baking. Lightly oil and line the base of an 18 cm/7 inch deep round cake tin with lightly oiled greaseproof or baking paper.

In a saucepan, gently heat the butter, sugar and honey until the butter has just melted.

Sift the flour, bicarbonate of soda and mixed spice together into a bowl.

Beat the egg and the milk until mixed thoroughly.

Make a well in the centre of the sifted flour and pour in the melted butter and honey. Using a wooden spoon, beat well, gradually drawing in the flour from the sides of the bowl. When all the flour has been beaten in, add the egg mixture and mix thoroughly. Pour into the prepared tin and sprinkle with the flaked almonds.

Bake in the preheated oven for 30–35 minutes, or until well risen and golden brown and a skewer inserted into the centre of the cake comes out clean. Remove from the oven, cool for a few minutes in the tin before turning out and leaving to cool on a wire rack. Drizzle with the remaining tablespoon of honey and serve.

Index